ChatGPT For Business

The Best Artificial Intelligence Applications, Marketing and Tools to boost your Income

Introduction

In the rapidly evolving landscape of modern business, staying ahead of the curve means embracing innovative technologies that can drive growth, enhance customer experiences, and streamline operations. One such technology that has emerged as a game-changer is Conversational AI, and at the forefront of this revolution stands ChatGPT - a cutting-edge language model developed by OpenAI.

"The Power of Conversational AI: Transforming Business with ChatGPT" is a comprehensive exploration of how businesses can harness the capabilities of ChatGPT to achieve unprecedented levels of efficiency, engagement, and success. This book serves as a strategic guide for business leaders, entrepreneurs, and professionals across industries who are eager to leverage the potential of Conversational AI to drive tangible outcomes.

In this book, we delve into the multifaceted world of Conversational AI, breaking down complex concepts into accessible insights. We will explore how ChatGPT, with its natural language processing prowess, has evolved from basic chatbots into a sophisticated tool that can engage customers, assist employees, optimize processes, and even spark innovation. Through real-world examples and practical strategies, we will illustrate how ChatGPT can seamlessly integrate into various business functions, reshaping customer support, marketing, product development, and more.

As we journey through the pages, we will uncover the underlying technologies that empower ChatGPT, demystifying concepts such as neural networks, machine learning, and data training. We will also address the ethical considerations that come with deploying AI-powered conversational systems, highlighting the importance of transparency, fairness, and responsible AI practices.

Whether you're a small business owner seeking to enhance customer interactions or a corporate executive looking to streamline internal communication, this book will provide you with the knowledge and tools needed to navigate the world of Conversational AI. By the time you reach the final page, you will be equipped with a strategic mindset and actionable insights to harness the full potential of ChatGPT, revolutionizing the way you do business.

Join us on this transformative journey as we unlock the power of Conversational AI and discover how ChatGPT can reshape the future of your business.

1. Introduction to ChatGPT for Business

Overview of ChatGPT

In an era where digital interactions are becoming increasingly prevalent, businesses are seeking innovative ways to engage with their customers, optimize operations, and drive growth. One technology that has emerged as a catalyst for these transformations is ChatGPT – a powerful and versatile conversational AI model developed by OpenAI.

In this opening chapter, we embark on a journey of exploration into the world of ChatGPT and its profound implications for the business landscape. We'll unravel the essence of ChatGPT, delve into its capabilities, and examine the underlying technologies that empower its functionality.

We begin by understanding the fundamental capabilities of ChatGPT. From generating human-like responses to understanding context and intent, ChatGPT possesses the ability to engage in natural, dynamic conversations. We'll explore its aptitude for context retention and its remarkable proficiency in mimicking human language patterns, making it a versatile tool for businesses aiming to enhance customer experiences.

To fully grasp the significance of ChatGPT, we trace the evolution of conversational AI – from rudimentary chatbots to sophisticated neural language models. This evolution showcases how ChatGPT stands at the forefront of a technological breakthrough, enabling businesses to interact with customers and stakeholders in ways that were once thought to be the domain of human communication.

At the heart of ChatGPT lies a complex architecture powered by deep learning, neural networks, and large-scale data training. In this section, we demystify these technologies, providing a clear understanding of how ChatGPT processes information, generates responses, and adapts its behavior based on context.

Applications Across Industries:

The versatility of ChatGPT transcends industry boundaries. We explore a range of sectors – from e-commerce to healthcare, finance to entertainment – and examine how businesses in each domain can leverage ChatGPT to revolutionize customer interactions, automate tasks, and unlock new avenues for innovation.

Ethical Considerations and Responsible AI:

As businesses integrate ChatGPT into their operations, ethical considerations take center stage. We discuss the importance of responsible AI deployment, emphasizing transparency, bias mitigation, and data privacy. By addressing these concerns, businesses can harness the power of ChatGPT while upholding ethical standards.

This chapter sets the stage for an in-depth exploration of ChatGPT's transformative potential for businesses. As we venture into subsequent chapters, we will delve deeper into specific use cases, strategies, and implementation guidelines, ensuring that you, the reader, are equipped with the knowledge and insights needed to navigate the dynamic landscape of Conversational AI and make informed decisions for your business's success.

The Importance of ChatGPT for Business

In an era defined by rapid technological advancement and evolving consumer expectations, businesses are under constant pressure to innovate and adapt. At the heart of this transformation lies the increasing importance of ChatGPT – a revolutionary conversational AI model that is reshaping the way businesses interact with their customers, employees, and stakeholders.

Enhancing Customer Experiences:

At the core of any successful business lies the ability to create memorable and meaningful customer experiences. ChatGPT serves as an invaluable tool in this pursuit. By providing personalized and responsive interactions around the clock, businesses can elevate customer satisfaction and loyalty. Whether it's addressing queries, offering recommendations, or assisting with purchases, ChatGPT ensures that customers feel heard and valued.

24/7 Availability and Scalability:

Traditional customer support has its limitations, with fixed hours of operation and the risk of long wait times. ChatGPT breaks down these barriers by offering round-the-clock availability. This scalability allows businesses to accommodate a global audience and manage high volumes of inquiries efficiently, without compromising on quality.

Empowering Employee Productivity:

Beyond customer-facing applications, ChatGPT can streamline internal processes and empower employees. It serves as a digital assistant capable of handling routine tasks, answering common queries, and providing quick access to information. This not only frees up employee time for more strategic activities but also ensures consistent and accurate responses across the organization.

Data-Driven Insights:

ChatGPT's interactions generate a wealth of data that can be leveraged for actionable insights. Businesses can analyze user interactions to identify trends, pain points, and emerging opportunities. These insights can drive informed decision-making, enabling businesses to refine their strategies and tailor their offerings to better meet customer needs.

Innovative Marketing and Engagement:

In the digital age, engagement is key to maintaining a brand's relevance. ChatGPT can be harnessed for innovative marketing campaigns, interactive content creation, and personalized recommendations. By offering users a dynamic and engaging experience, businesses can foster stronger connections and drive brand loyalty.

Unlocking New Avenues for Creativity:

ChatGPT's ability to generate human-like text extends beyond functional interactions. It can be harnessed as a creative tool for content generation, brainstorming sessions, and idea exploration. Businesses can tap into its capabilities to generate product descriptions, social media posts, blog articles, and more.

Staying Ahead of the Curve:

The adoption of ChatGPT positions businesses at the forefront of technological innovation. As competitors adapt and consumers evolve, businesses that embrace Conversational AI gain a competitive edge. By being early adopters, these businesses position themselves to meet the changing demands of the market effectively.

In this chapter, we've explored the multifaceted ways in which ChatGPT is reshaping the business landscape. Its impact extends far beyond customer service, permeating various aspects of operations, marketing, and innovation. As we continue our journey through this book, we'll delve into actionable strategies and real-world examples that highlight how businesses can harness the full potential of ChatGPT to drive growth, efficiency, and success.

Benefits of Integrating ChatGPT in Business Operations

In a world where seamless communication and operational efficiency reign supreme, businesses are turning to innovative solutions to optimize their processes. Among these solutions, integrating ChatGPT into various aspects of business operations stands out as a transformative strategy. In this chapter, we delve into the myriad benefits that businesses can reap by leveraging ChatGPT to enhance their operations.

1. Enhanced Customer Support and Engagement:

Integrating ChatGPT into customer support functions can lead to faster response times, personalized interactions, and consistent service quality. Customers receive immediate assistance, leading to increased satisfaction and loyalty. The model's ability to understand and adapt to context ensures that customers feel heard and understood.

2. Automation of Routine Tasks:

Businesses can offload routine and repetitive tasks to ChatGPT, allowing employees to focus on higher-value activities. Whether it's answering frequently asked questions, processing simple transactions, or guiding users through basic troubleshooting, ChatGPT's automation capabilities save time and resources.

3. Scalability and Availability:

ChatGPT operates 24/7, catering to customers across different time zones and reducing the need for extensive human staffing. This scalability ensures that businesses can handle spikes in customer interactions without compromising on service quality.

4. Consistent and Accurate Information:

By centralizing information and responses, ChatGPT ensures that customers receive consistent and accurate information across all touchpoints. This minimizes the risk of misinformation and enhances the credibility of the business.

5. Data-Driven Insights and Analysis:

Interactions with ChatGPT generate a wealth of data that can provide valuable insights into customer behavior, preferences, and pain points. Businesses can analyze this data to refine their strategies, identify trends, and tailor their offerings to better match customer needs.

6. Personalized Recommendations:

ChatGPT's ability to understand user preferences and behaviors allows businesses to offer personalized recommendations. Whether it's suggesting products, services, or content, these recommendations enhance user experiences and drive conversion rates.

7. Streamlined Internal Communication:

ChatGPT isn't limited to customer interactions. It can also serve as an internal communication tool, assisting employees with queries, facilitating knowledge sharing, and streamlining information retrieval within the organization.

8. Innovation and Ideation:

Businesses can leverage ChatGPT's text generation capabilities for brainstorming sessions, creative content creation, and idea generation. This fosters a culture of innovation and encourages employees to think outside the box.

9. Multilingual Support:

ChatGPT's proficiency in multiple languages allows businesses to engage with diverse customer bases without the need for extensive language resources. This expands market reach and fosters inclusivity.

10. Competitive Edge and Future-Readiness:

By integrating ChatGPT into their operations, businesses position themselves at the forefront of technological innovation. This adaptability demonstrates an ability to embrace emerging trends and stay relevant in a rapidly evolving business landscape.

As we explore the practical strategies and use cases in the following chapters, the benefits of integrating ChatGPT into business operations will become even clearer. By harnessing its capabilities, businesses can optimize their processes, engage with customers more effectively, and position themselves for sustained success in the digital age.

Ethical Considerations:

Addressing Potential Concerns about AI-Generated Content

In the pursuit of innovation and efficiency, businesses must navigate the ethical landscape of AI-generated content. As ChatGPT and similar technologies become integral to operations, it's essential to address the potential concerns that arise from the use of AI in content creation, customer interactions, and decision-making processes. In this chapter, we delve into the ethical considerations that businesses must grapple with and provide insights into responsible AI deployment.

Transparency and Disclosure:

Businesses must be transparent about the involvement of AI in customer interactions. Users have a right to know whether they are engaging with a human or an AI-powered system. Providing clear disclosure maintains trust and ensures that users are fully informed about the nature of their interactions.

Bias Mitigation:

AI models like ChatGPT learn from vast amounts of data, which can inadvertently encode biases present in the data. Businesses need to implement strategies to identify and mitigate biases that might emerge in AI-generated content, ensuring fairness and equal treatment across diverse user groups.

Data Privacy and Security:

Interactions with AI systems often involve the sharing of sensitive information. Businesses must prioritize data privacy and implement robust security measures to protect user data from breaches or unauthorized access. This includes adhering to relevant data protection regulations.

User Consent and Control:

Users should have control over the extent to which their data is used and shared in AI-powered interactions. Businesses must obtain clear consent for data usage and provide users with options to modify or delete their data if desired.

Avoiding Misleading Content:

AI-generated content should be designed to avoid misleading users. Businesses should ensure that the information provided by AI systems is accurate, fact-based, and does not create false impressions or expectations.

Human Oversight and Intervention:

While AI can handle a wide range of tasks, there should be mechanisms in place for human oversight and intervention. This ensures that critical decisions or sensitive interactions are supervised by humans to prevent errors or inappropriate responses.

Responsible Content Generation:

AI models like ChatGPT have the ability to generate text that can influence opinions and emotions. Businesses should exercise caution when using AI to generate content that could have a significant impact on users, ensuring that the content aligns with ethical guidelines and organizational values.

Continuous Monitoring and Improvement:

AI systems should be continually monitored for any unintended behaviors or outcomes. Regular assessment helps identify issues and allows for timely adjustments to ensure responsible and ethical AI deployment.

Education and Training:

Businesses should invest in educating their teams about AI ethics and responsible AI practices. Employees interacting with AI systems should understand the ethical implications and be equipped to handle potential challenges.

Regulatory Compliance:

As AI technologies evolve, regulatory frameworks may emerge to address their ethical implications. Businesses must stay informed about relevant regulations and ensure compliance with emerging standards.

In a rapidly changing technological landscape, businesses that prioritize ethical considerations in their AI initiatives not only build trust with their customers but also contribute to the responsible development and deployment of AI technologies. By addressing these ethical concerns head-on, businesses can harness the benefits of AI-generated content while upholding their commitment to integrity, fairness, and user well-being.

Ensuring Responsible and Ethical Usage of ChatGPT in Business Contexts

As businesses integrate ChatGPT into their operations, ensuring responsible and ethical usage of this powerful tool becomes paramount. This chapter delves into practical guidelines and strategies that businesses can adopt to uphold ethical standards and navigate the complex landscape of AI deployment.

1. Establish Clear Ethical Guidelines:

Develop a comprehensive set of ethical guidelines that outline the principles and values guiding the use of ChatGPT. These guidelines should cover areas such as transparency, data privacy, bias mitigation, and user consent.

2. Transparency in AI Interactions:

Ensure that users are informed when they are interacting with an AI system. Transparently disclose the AI's role in customer interactions to maintain honesty and trust.

3. Regular Audits and Assessments:

Conduct regular audits of AI-generated content to identify potential biases, inaccuracies, or unintended outcomes. Regular assessments help in fine-tuning the AI system and addressing ethical concerns promptly.

4. Bias Mitigation Strategies:

Implement mechanisms to identify and mitigate biases in AI-generated content. This involves careful data selection, preprocessing, and ongoing monitoring to ensure fairness and inclusivity.

5. Data Privacy and Security Measures:

Prioritize data privacy by implementing robust security measures to protect user data. Comply with data protection regulations and ensure that user data is handled responsibly.

6. User Consent and Control:

Obtain clear and informed consent from users for the usage of their data in AI interactions. Provide options for users to control their data and its usage.

7. Human Oversight and Intervention:

Integrate human oversight and intervention in critical decision-making processes. Human experts should be available to review and approve AI-generated content in sensitive situations.

8. Continual Training and Education:

Educate employees about AI ethics, responsible usage, and potential pitfalls. Training ensures that employees understand the ethical considerations and can identify and address any issues that arise.

9. Responsive to Feedback and Complaints:

Create channels for users to provide feedback on AI interactions. Actively address user concerns and continuously improve the AI system based on feedback.

10. Collaboration with Ethical Experts:

Engage with ethicists, AI researchers, and professionals in the field to gain insights into ethical best practices. Collaboration can help refine your ethical guidelines and strategies.

11. Adapting to Regulatory Changes:

Stay informed about evolving regulations related to AI and adapt your ethical practices accordingly. Regulatory compliance ensures that your AI initiatives align with legal requirements.

12. Transparency in Content Generation:

Clearly label AI-generated content as such, particularly in scenarios where users might mistake it for human-generated content. This transparency prevents confusion and misrepresentation.

13. Responsible Marketing and Branding:

Ensure that any marketing or branding efforts involving AI-generated content are accurate and do not create false impressions. Transparency extends to how you present AI-driven capabilities to your audience.

By integrating these guidelines into your business's AI deployment strategy, you can proactively address ethical concerns and demonstrate your commitment to responsible AI usage. This not only safeguards your reputation but also contributes to the overall responsible development and adoption of AI technologies in the business landscape.

2. Leveraging ChatGPT for Marketing

Personalized Customer Engagement

Creating Tailored Marketing Messages with ChatGPT

In the dynamic world of marketing, where the attention of consumers is a valuable commodity, businesses are constantly seeking innovative ways to create deeper connections and resonate with their target audience. Enter ChatGPT – a potent tool that opens new avenues for personalized customer engagement. In this chapter, we explore how businesses can leverage ChatGPT to craft compelling and personalized marketing messages that captivate, engage, and convert.

The Power of Personalization:

Personalization lies at the heart of effective marketing. Customers are more likely to engage with content that feels tailor-made for their needs and preferences. ChatGPT empowers businesses to take personalization to new heights by generating content that speaks directly to individual consumers.

Understanding Consumer Insights:

ChatGPT can analyze consumer data to gain insights into preferences, browsing behavior, and purchasing history. By understanding what customers are looking for, businesses can create marketing messages that align with their interests.

Crafting Dynamic Conversations:

ChatGPT is not limited to one-size-fits-all messaging. It can initiate dynamic conversations with consumers, asking questions, seeking feedback, and adapting its responses based on user input. This interactive approach engages customers in meaningful dialogues that foster a sense of connection.

Tailoring Content to Buyer Personas:

Businesses often segment their audience into different buyer personas – fictionalized representations of different customer types. ChatGPT can craft marketing messages that align with each persona's unique characteristics, ensuring relevance and resonance.

Seamless Content Creation:

ChatGPT can swiftly generate a variety of content types – from social media posts and blog articles to email subject lines and product descriptions. This streamlines content creation and frees up marketing teams to focus on strategy and creativity.

Creating Compelling Recommendations:

ChatGPT's ability to understand consumer preferences allows businesses to offer personalized recommendations. Whether suggesting products, services, or content, these recommendations enhance user experiences and drive conversions.

A/B Testing and Iterative Refinement:

Marketing is an iterative process, and ChatGPT can accelerate this cycle. Create multiple variations of marketing messages, test them using A/B testing, and use the insights gained to refine your approach continually.

Human-Touch Amplification:

While ChatGPT can generate content, businesses can inject a human touch by reviewing and fine-tuning the AI-generated messages. This ensures that the content maintains authenticity and reflects the brand's voice.

Building Lasting Relationships:

Personalized marketing messages foster deeper connections between businesses and consumers. By showing that you understand their needs and preferences, you lay the foundation for long-term relationships and brand loyalty.

Ethical Considerations:

While personalization is powerful, businesses must ensure that data privacy and user consent are paramount. Transparently communicate how user data will be used to create personalized messages and provide options for users to opt out if desired.

As we journey further into this chapter, we will delve into practical strategies, examples, and best practices that highlight the intricate art of creating personalized marketing messages with ChatGPT. By mastering the balance between automation and human touch, businesses can build stronger customer relationships and drive meaningful engagement.

Enhancing Customer Interactions through Tailored Content

In the ever-evolving landscape of customer interactions, the ability to deliver tailored content is a key differentiator for businesses seeking to create memorable experiences. ChatGPT offers a revolutionary approach to enhancing these interactions by generating personalized and relevant content that resonates with individual customers. In this section, we dive deeper into the strategies and techniques that businesses can employ to enhance customer engagement through ChatGPT-generated tailored content.

Mapping Customer Journeys:

Understanding the customer journey is fundamental to delivering tailored content. ChatGPT can analyze customer touchpoints and interactions, helping businesses identify critical moments where personalized content can make a significant impact.

Segmentation and Persona-Based Content:

Segment your audience into distinct groups and develop detailed buyer personas for each segment. ChatGPT can then create content that speaks directly to the unique needs, challenges, and aspirations of each persona.

Dynamic Email Campaigns:

Email marketing remains a potent tool, and ChatGPT can elevate its impact. Craft dynamic email campaigns that adapt based on user interactions, ensuring that customers receive content aligned with their preferences.

Contextual Website Experiences:

Personalize website experiences by integrating ChatGPT-generated content. This includes dynamic landing pages, tailored product recommendations, and content suggestions that evolve as users navigate the site.

Social Media Engagement:

Social media platforms offer a prime opportunity for personalized interactions. ChatGPT can generate posts, comments, and responses that resonate with individual users, fostering engagement and interactions.

Real-Time Customer Support:

Embed ChatGPT into customer support channels for instant and personalized assistance. The model can understand inquiries, provide relevant information, and even guide customers through troubleshooting processes.

Product Recommendations and Upselling:

Leverage ChatGPT to suggest complementary products or services based on a customer's previous purchases or preferences. These tailored recommendations can drive upselling and cross-selling opportunities.

Localized and Cultural Sensitivity:

ChatGPT can adapt content based on geographic location and cultural nuances. This ensures that the content feels relevant and respectful to customers across different regions.

Content Consistency and Quality:

ChatGPT-generated content should maintain the same level of quality and consistency as human-generated content. Regularly review and refine the AI-generated content to align with your brand voice and style.

Feedback Integration:

ChatGPT can actively seek feedback from customers and use this input to generate personalized content. This interactive approach demonstrates responsiveness and a commitment to meeting customer needs.

Monitoring and Iteration:

Continuously monitor customer interactions and gather data on how users engage with the tailored content. Use these insights to refine your strategies and make data-driven improvements.

Ethical Usage and Data Privacy:

As always, prioritize ethical considerations and data privacy. Obtain user consent for content personalization, clearly communicate how data will be used, and allow users to opt out if desired.

By embracing the capabilities of ChatGPT for generating tailored content, businesses can forge deeper connections with customers, drive engagement, and cultivate a sense of loyalty. As we proceed, we will delve into real-world examples and delve further into the execution of these strategies, equipping you with the tools to revolutionize your customer interactions.

Content Generation:

Automating Content Creation for Blogs, Social Media, and Emails
In an era where content consumption is at an all-time high, businesses face the challenge of consistently producing engaging content for blogs, social media platforms, and email campaigns. ChatGPT emerges as a transformative solution, offering the ability to automate content creation across these channels while maintaining quality and relevance. In this section, we delve into the strategies and techniques that businesses can employ to harness the power of ChatGPT for automated content generation.

Blogging Made Effortless:

Generating blog posts can be time-consuming, but ChatGPT streamlines the process. Provide the AI with a topic or a brief, and it can generate well-structured, informative, and engaging blog posts in a fraction of the time.

1. Defining Topics and Guidelines:

Clearly outline the topic and guidelines for the blog post. Specify the tone, style, and key points you want to be included in the content.

2. Generating Drafts:

ChatGPT can create an initial draft of the blog post. While the initial draft may require review and refinement, it serves as a strong starting point.

3. Refining and Personalizing:

Human content creators can review and edit the draft to ensure it aligns with the brand voice and style. Add personal touches, examples, and insights to enhance the content's authenticity.

4. SEO Optimization:

Integrate relevant keywords and ensure that the content is optimized for search engines. This boosts the visibility of the blog post in search results.

5. Consistent Posting Schedule:

Use ChatGPT to generate a backlog of blog posts, ensuring a consistent posting schedule that keeps your audience engaged.

Social Media Magic:

Social media platforms demand frequent updates and engaging content. ChatGPT can help businesses maintain an active online presence with automated social media posts.

1. Crafting Eye-Catching Posts:

Specify the platform (e.g., Twitter, Facebook, Instagram) and the nature of the post (e.g., announcement, tip, question). ChatGPT can generate short and attention-grabbing posts.

2. Incorporating Hashtags and Emojis:

Leverage relevant hashtags and emojis to enhance the reach and engagement of your social media posts.

3. Adapting to Trends:

Stay current by having ChatGPT generate posts related to trending topics or events in real-time.

Email Campaigns Refined:

Email marketing remains a valuable channel for customer engagement. ChatGPT can automate the creation of email subject lines and body content.

1. Personalizing Subject Lines:

ChatGPT can create subject lines that resonate with each recipient, increasing the likelihood of email opens.

2. Crafting Compelling Content:

Automate the creation of email body content, tailoring messages based on recipient preferences, purchase history, or interactions.

3. A/B Testing Variations:

Generate different versions of subject lines and email content using ChatGPT. Test these variations to identify the most effective combinations.

4. Segmented Campaigns:

Use ChatGPT to create email content specific to different customer segments, enhancing relevance and engagement.

Ethical Considerations:

While ChatGPT can automate content creation, ensure that the content aligns with your brand values and maintains authenticity. Regular human oversight and review are crucial to ensuring the content's quality and relevance.

By integrating ChatGPT into your content generation strategy, you can streamline the process, maintain a consistent online presence, and free up your creative teams to focus on higher-level strategies. As we delve further, we will explore hands-on approaches and real-world examples that demonstrate the transformative impact of automated content creation on your marketing efforts.

Maintaining consistent and high-quality content output

Consistency and quality are the cornerstones of effective content marketing. While automation with ChatGPT offers the potential to streamline content creation, ensuring a balance between quantity and quality is paramount. In this section, we explore strategies to maintain a steady flow of content while upholding high standards using ChatGPT.

Content Calendar Planning:

Develop a content calendar that outlines the topics, formats, and publishing schedule. ChatGPT can generate content based on this calendar, ensuring a steady output.

1. Defining Themes and Topics:

Determine overarching themes and specific topics for each content piece. Provide these to ChatGPT to ensure content aligns with your marketing strategy.

2. Batch Content Creation:

Utilize ChatGPT to create batches of content in advance. This approach ensures a consistent stream of content even during busy periods.

3. Review and Quality Control:

Assign a content editor or reviewer to ensure that AI-generated content meets your brand's quality standards. Edit and enhance the content for authenticity.

4. Customization for Platforms:

While ChatGPT can generate content, tailor it for specific platforms. Content might need adjustment for blog posts, social media, or email campaigns.

Topic Research and Trend Analysis:

Use ChatGPT to research trending topics, industry insights, and user preferences. This data can guide your content strategy and ensure relevance.

1. Gathering Insights:

Ask ChatGPT to provide insights into current industry trends, consumer behaviors, or emerging topics.

2. Crafting Thought Leadership:

Leverage the AI's insights to create thought leadership content that positions your brand as an authority in your industry.

Content Variations and Adaptations:

Generate variations of AI-generated content to cater to different segments or platforms. Customization maintains engagement and relevance.

1. Tailoring for Audiences:

Adjust content based on audience demographics, preferences, and needs to ensure it resonates effectively.

2. Multilingual Content:

ChatGPT's multilingual capabilities allow you to create content for diverse markets, expanding your global reach.

Incorporating User Feedback:

Collect feedback from users and integrate it into AI-generated content. This fosters a sense of collaboration and user involvement.

1. User-Generated Ideas:

Ask ChatGPT to generate content based on user feedback or questions received through various channels.

2. Showcasing Customer Stories:

Use AI-generated content to share success stories or testimonials from customers, further building trust and credibility.

Refining and Iteration:

AI-generated content can evolve over time. Continuously refine your AI's training data and adjust prompts for improved output.

1. Learning from Analytics:

Analyze engagement metrics and user responses to understand which AI-generated content performs best and resonates with your audience.

2. Feedback Loop with the AI:

Use the AI's generated content as a basis for feedback and improvement. Over time, this loop enhances the AI's content accuracy and alignment.

Ethical and Brand Consistency:

While AI-generated content is a valuable tool, ensure that it aligns with your brand voice and values. Maintain a balance between automation and human touch to preserve authenticity.

By blending ChatGPT's content generation capabilities with human oversight and strategic planning, businesses can maintain a consistent content output without compromising quality. As we move forward, we'll delve into real-world examples and practical implementations to illustrate the harmonious integration of automation and human expertise in content marketing.

Customer Support and Service:

Utilizing ChatGPT for Real-Time Customer Support

Exceptional customer support is a cornerstone of successful businesses. With the advent of ChatGPT, real-time customer support can be taken to new heights. This section delves into the strategies and techniques for leveraging ChatGPT to provide efficient and effective customer support that meets the evolving needs of your customers.

Instant Responses 24/7:

ChatGPT's availability around the clock ensures that customers can get answers to their queries instantly, regardless of the time of day.

1. Quick Query Resolution:

ChatGPT can handle routine and frequently asked questions, providing immediate responses to common inquiries.

2. Basic Troubleshooting:

Guide customers through simple troubleshooting steps for common issues, resolving problems without delay.

Personalized Interactions:

ChatGPT can analyze customer profiles and interactions to provide personalized assistance that feels tailored to each customer.

1. Addressing User History:

Use previous interactions and purchase history to offer personalized recommendations, enhancing the user experience.

2. Contextual Conversations:

ChatGPT's ability to retain context allows for seamless and natural conversations, mimicking human interactions.

Handling High Volume:

During peak times, customer inquiries can surge. ChatGPT's scalability ensures that no customer is left waiting for a response.

1. Efficient Queue Management:

ChatGPT can manage multiple customer inquiries simultaneously, minimizing wait times for everyone.

2. Temporary Surges in Traffic:

Scale up ChatGPT's capacity during marketing promotions or special events to handle temporary spikes in customer queries.

Multilingual Support:

ChatGPT's language capabilities allow you to provide customer support in various languages, catering to a diverse customer base.

1. Expanding Global Reach:

Offer customer support to international customers without the need for extensive language resources.

2. Localized Assistance:

Address cultural nuances and regional preferences to provide a more personalized and relatable support experience.

Escalation to Human Agents:

While ChatGPT is adept at handling routine queries, it can seamlessly escalate complex issues to human support agents.

1. Human Oversight:

Ensure that critical inquiries are reviewed and resolved by trained human agents to prevent errors or misunderstandings.

2. Collaborative Problem Solving:

Create a symbiotic relationship between ChatGPT and human agents, utilizing the strengths of both for optimal customer solutions.

Real-Time Updates and Notifications:

Utilize ChatGPT to provide real-time updates on order statuses, service changes, or important announcements.

1. Timely Communication:

Keep customers informed about the latest developments, ensuring transparency and trust.

2. Automated Notifications:

Use ChatGPT to automate notifications, reducing the workload of customer support teams.

Ethical Considerations:

Prioritize data privacy and ensure that customer data is handled responsibly. Transparently communicate how customer data is used in interactions and adhere to relevant data protection regulations.

By integrating ChatGPT into your customer support strategy, businesses can provide efficient, personalized, and round-the-clock assistance that enhances customer satisfaction and loyalty. As we move forward, we will delve into real-world scenarios and practical applications that showcase the power of ChatGPT in revolutionizing customer support and service.

Streamlining Query Resolution and Issue Handling

In the world of customer support, efficiency and accuracy are paramount. ChatGPT can revolutionize query resolution and issue handling, ensuring swift and effective assistance for customers. This section explores strategies and techniques to harness ChatGPT's capabilities for seamless problem-solving and streamlined customer interactions.

Swift and Accurate Responses:

ChatGPT's rapid processing allows for immediate responses, minimizing customer wait times and frustration.

1. Automated Responses:

Utilize ChatGPT to provide quick answers to common queries, resolving issues without human intervention.

2. Rapid Triage:

Automatically categorize and prioritize inquiries, directing urgent issues to human agents while handling routine matters with ChatGPT.

Guided Troubleshooting:

ChatGPT can walk customers through troubleshooting steps, helping them resolve simple issues on their own.

1. Step-by-Step Instructions:

Provide clear and concise instructions for users to follow, leading them to a resolution.

2. Interactive Problem-Solving:

Engage customers in a conversational manner, adapting responses based on their input to guide them to solutions.

Efficient Issue Escalation:

ChatGPT can identify complex issues and seamlessly escalate them to human agents for in-depth assistance.

1. Intelligent Triaging:

Utilize AI to assess the complexity of an issue and determine if it requires human intervention.

2. Agent Collaboration:

ChatGPT can provide context and preliminary information to human agents, expediting issue resolution.

Multi-Platform Support:

Deploy ChatGPT across various communication channels, such as websites, mobile apps, and messaging platforms.

1. Omni-Channel Assistance:

Offer consistent support experiences regardless of where customers reach out, ensuring a cohesive support journey.

2. Interactive Chat Widgets:

Integrate ChatGPT-powered chat widgets on websites for real-time assistance and increased customer engagement.

Seamless Handoffs:

When human intervention is needed, ChatGPT can provide background information to human agents for smooth transitions.

1. Context Preservation:

Ensure that customer context is transferred to human agents, avoiding repetition and enhancing the user experience.

2. Reduced Agent Load:

Human agents can focus on resolving complex issues, while ChatGPT handles routine queries.

Data-Driven Insights:

Analyze interactions with ChatGPT to identify trends and pain points, enabling proactive improvements.

1. Continuous Improvement:

Regularly refine ChatGPT's responses based on user feedback and data insights to enhance accuracy and relevance.

2. Customer Feedback Loop:

Gather user input on the effectiveness of ChatGPT interactions to iterate and optimize the support process.

Ethical Considerations:

Transparently communicate to users when they are interacting with an AI-powered system. Prioritize data privacy and ensure user consent for interactions.

By integrating ChatGPT into your customer support infrastructure, businesses can streamline query resolution and issue handling, delivering efficient and effective solutions that foster customer satisfaction and loyalty. As we proceed, we will explore practical implementations and real-world scenarios that highlight the transformative impact of ChatGPT in elevating customer support processes.

3. Best Tools and Practices

Choosing the Right Platform

Selecting the optimal platform is a pivotal step in effectively integrating ChatGPT into your business operations. This chapter delves into the considerations, criteria, and best practices for choosing the right platform to leverage the power of ChatGPT for your specific business needs.

Understanding Your Objectives:

Before choosing a platform, define your objectives. Are you looking to enhance customer support, automate content creation, or drive personalized marketing? Understanding your goals will guide your platform selection.

Scalability and Availability:

Evaluate platforms that offer the scalability and availability needed to handle your anticipated volume of interactions. Ensure that the platform can accommodate growth and peak usage.

Integration Capabilities:

Choose a platform that seamlessly integrates with your existing systems, such as customer relationship management (CRM) tools, content management systems (CMS), and e-commerce platforms.

Natural Language Understanding:

Assess the platform's natural language understanding capabilities. Look for models like ChatGPT that can comprehend context, nuances, and user intent effectively.

Multilingual Support:

Consider whether the platform supports multiple languages, especially if your business caters to an international audience. Multilingual capabilities can enhance global engagement.

Customization and Training:

Opt for a platform that allows you to fine-tune the AI model to better align with your brand voice, industry terminology, and user interactions.

Data Privacy and Security:

Prioritize platforms that adhere to robust data privacy and security standards. Ensure that customer data is protected and handled responsibly.

Ease of Use and Deployment:

Choose a user-friendly platform that enables easy deployment without extensive technical expertise. An intuitive interface can expedite integration and implementation.

Human-Agent Collaboration:

Evaluate whether the platform facilitates seamless collaboration between AI-powered systems like ChatGPT and human agents for complex queries and support.

Support and Maintenance:

Select a platform that offers reliable customer support and regular updates. Ensure that you have access to resources for troubleshooting and assistance.

Cost and Value:

Assess the cost structure of the platform in relation to the value it provides. Consider factors like licensing fees, usage charges, and return on investment.

Testing and Evaluation:

Before committing to a platform, conduct thorough testing and evaluation. Test its performance, response accuracy, and ability to meet your business goals.

Vendor Reputation and Reviews:

Research the reputation of the platform vendor and seek feedback from other businesses that have used the platform. User reviews and testimonials can provide valuable insights.

Ethical Considerations:

Ensure that the platform aligns with your ethical guidelines and values. Transparent communication and responsible AI practices should be fundamental.

Future-Readiness:

Choose a platform that is adaptable and capable of accommodating emerging AI advancements and business requirements.

By carefully considering these factors and aligning them with your business goals, you can make an informed decision when selecting the right platform for integrating ChatGPT. As we continue through this chapter, we will explore further tools and best practices that empower you to harness the full potential of ChatGPT in various aspects of your business.

Overview of Platforms Supporting ChatGPT Integration

In the rapidly evolving landscape of AI integration, several platforms offer support for seamlessly incorporating ChatGPT into your business operations. This section provides an overview of some prominent platforms that facilitate the integration of ChatGPT, enabling you to enhance customer engagement, streamline processes, and drive innovation.

1. OpenAI API:

The OpenAI API provides direct access to the power of ChatGPT, allowing you to integrate its capabilities into your applications, websites, and services. With versatile customization options and the ability to fine-tune the model, the OpenAI API offers a high degree of control over AI interactions.

2. Third-Party Integration Platforms:

Several third-party platforms offer pre-built integrations for ChatGPT. These platforms often provide user-friendly interfaces, making it easier to deploy ChatGPT for specific use cases like customer support, content creation, and marketing.

3. Cloud Service Providers:

Major cloud service providers, such as Amazon Web Services (AWS) and Microsoft Azure, offer AI services that can integrate ChatGPT. These platforms provide scalable infrastructure and tools to deploy and manage AI models effectively.

4. Chatbot Frameworks:

Various chatbot frameworks, such as Microsoft Bot Framework, Dialogflow by Google, and Rasa, allow you to integrate ChatGPT into chatbot applications. These frameworks provide tools for creating conversational agents with AI capabilities.

5. Content Management Systems (CMS):

Some CMS platforms offer plugins or integrations that enable seamless content creation and management using ChatGPT. These integrations can automate content generation, ensuring a steady flow of high-quality content.

6. E-commerce Platforms:

E-commerce platforms may offer extensions or integrations that leverage ChatGPT for personalized product recommendations, customer support, and interactive shopping experiences.

7. Customer Support Tools:

Certain customer support tools incorporate AI-driven chatbots, including ChatGPT, to enhance real-time query resolution and issue handling. These tools often integrate with existing customer support systems.

8. Marketing Automation Platforms:

Marketing automation platforms may integrate ChatGPT to automate content creation, tailor marketing messages, and personalize customer interactions across various channels.

9. API Marketplaces:

Explore API marketplaces that offer ChatGPT as a service, allowing you to integrate AI-generated content and interactions into your applications without extensive development effort.

10. Custom-built Solutions:

For businesses with specific requirements, custom-built solutions can be developed to integrate ChatGPT directly into proprietary systems, applications, or processes.

When selecting a platform for ChatGPT integration, consider factors such as ease of use, customization capabilities, scalability, integration options, and the specific use case your business aims to address. Each platform may offer unique features and benefits that align with your goals, enabling you to harness the full potential of ChatGPT in enhancing your business operations.

Data Privacy and Security

As businesses integrate ChatGPT into their operations, data privacy and security must remain paramount. This section explores the critical considerations, best practices, and tools to ensure that the integration of ChatGPT aligns with robust data protection measures and safeguards sensitive information.

User Data Handling:

Implement clear guidelines for how user data will be used in interactions with ChatGPT. Ensure that data is collected, stored, and processed in compliance with relevant data protection regulations.

1. Consent Management:

Obtain explicit user consent for data usage in AI interactions. Provide clear information about the purpose of data collection and offer opt-out options.

2. Data Minimization:

Collect only the necessary data required for interactions, minimizing the exposure of sensitive information.

Data Encryption:

Utilize strong encryption protocols to protect data in transit and at rest, preventing unauthorized access or data breaches.

1. SSL/TLS:

Implement Secure Socket Layer (SSL) or Transport Layer Security (TLS) encryption for data transmitted between users and the AI system.

2. Encryption at Rest:

Encrypt stored data to ensure that even if data is compromised, it remains unintelligible without the appropriate decryption keys.

Access Control and Authorization:

Control access to data and AI systems, ensuring that only authorized personnel can interact with and manage sensitive information.

1. Role-Based Access:

Assign specific roles and permissions to individuals based on their responsibilities, limiting access to sensitive data.

2. Multi-Factor Authentication:

Implement multi-factor authentication for accessing AI platforms and systems, adding an extra layer of security.

Regular Audits and Monitoring:

Conduct regular security audits and monitoring to detect and address vulnerabilities or suspicious activities promptly.

1. Intrusion Detection Systems (IDS):

Deploy IDS to identify and respond to any unauthorized attempts to access data or the AI system.

2. Log Analysis:

Analyze logs to track interactions, identify anomalies, and ensure that AI-generated content aligns with ethical and security standards.

Vendor Security Assessment:

When using third-party platforms for ChatGPT integration, assess the security measures and practices of the chosen vendor.

1. Data Processing Agreements (DPAs):

Ensure that vendors provide DPAs that outline how they handle data, maintain security, and comply with relevant regulations.

2. Compliance with Standards:

Choose vendors that adhere to industry standards and certifications for data security, such as ISO 27001 or SOC 2.

User Anonymization and Consent:

Anonymize user data whenever possible, and ensure that AI interactions respect user preferences and consent.

1. Opt-Out Mechanisms:

Allow users to opt out of data collection or AI interactions if they wish to maintain their privacy.

2. Data Retention Policies:

Define clear policies for how long user data will be retained and when it will be permanently deleted.

By incorporating these data privacy and security practices into the ChatGPT integration process, businesses can foster trust, protect user information, and demonstrate their commitment to responsible AI usage. As we continue exploring best tools and practices, you will gain insights into how to maintain a secure and ethical AI-powered environment.

Implementing Measures to Protect Customer Data

Protecting customer data is not only a legal requirement but also a fundamental ethical obligation. This section outlines concrete measures and best practices to implement robust safeguards for customer data when integrating ChatGPT into your business operations.

Data Encryption:

Encrypt customer data during transmission and storage to prevent unauthorized access or data breaches.

Use SSL/TLS Encryption: Implement Secure Socket Layer (SSL) or Transport Layer Security (TLS) encryption to secure data transmission between users and the AI system.

Encryption at Rest: Encrypt stored data to ensure its confidentiality, even if physical or digital access is compromised.

Access Control and Authorization:

Control who can access customer data and ensure that only authorized personnel have the necessary permissions.

Role-Based Access Control: Assign specific roles and access levels based on job responsibilities, limiting access to sensitive information.

Multi-Factor Authentication (MFA): Require multi-factor authentication for accessing platforms or systems that handle customer data.

Data Minimization:

Collect and store only the data that is necessary for AI interactions, reducing the risk of data exposure.

Limit Data Collection: Gather only the minimum required data for AI interactions, adhering to the principle of data minimization.

Regular Audits and Monitoring:

Conduct frequent security audits and monitoring to identify and address vulnerabilities promptly.

Intrusion Detection Systems (IDS): Deploy IDS to detect and respond to unauthorized attempts to access data or the AI system.

Log Analysis: Regularly analyze logs to track interactions, detect anomalies, and ensure compliance with security standards.

Vendor Assessment and Agreements:

Assess the security practices of any third-party platforms or vendors involved in the ChatGPT integration.

Data Processing Agreements (DPAs): Ensure vendors provide DPAs that outline data handling, security practices, and compliance with regulations.

Compliance with Standards: Choose vendors that adhere to recognized security standards and certifications.

Data Retention and Deletion:

Establish clear policies for retaining and deleting customer data to minimize the risk of data exposure.

Data Retention Policies: Define how long customer data will be retained and when it will be permanently deleted.

Secure Data Disposal: Ensure proper data disposal methods, including secure erasure or destruction of customer data when it is no longer needed.

User Consent and Transparency:

Obtain explicit user consent for data usage in AI interactions and provide transparent communication about data handling.

Opt-In/Opt-Out Mechanisms: Allow users to opt in or opt out of data collection and AI interactions based on their preferences.

Privacy Policies: Clearly communicate data handling practices and AI usage in your privacy policies.

By implementing these measures, businesses can create a secure environment for integrating ChatGPT while upholding data protection standards, building trust with customers, and maintaining ethical AI practices. As we progress, we will explore additional tools and practices to further enhance the responsible deployment of ChatGPT in your business operations.

Complying with Data Privacy Regulations

As businesses integrate ChatGPT into their operations, compliance with data privacy regulations is of utmost importance. This section provides a comprehensive guide on how to navigate data privacy regulations while effectively utilizing ChatGPT to enhance your business processes.

1. Understand Applicable Regulations:

Familiarize yourself with the data privacy regulations that apply to your business, such as the General Data Protection Regulation (GDPR), California Consumer Privacy Act (CCPA), or other regional regulations.

2. Data Mapping and Inventory:

Identify and document the types of data processed, collected, and stored during AI interactions, along with the purpose and legal basis for processing.

3. User Consent Management:

Obtain explicit and informed consent from users before processing their data in AI interactions.

Implement opt-in mechanisms that clearly explain the purpose of data processing and how AI will be involved.

Allow users to withdraw consent and provide mechanisms for opting out of data processing.

4. Transparency and Notices:

Ensure transparency by providing clear and concise privacy notices and terms of service that explain data processing, AI usage, and user rights.

Clearly communicate how AI interacts with user data and its role in enhancing user experience.

Inform users about their rights, including the right to access, rectify, and delete their data.

5. Data Minimization:

Collect and process only the data necessary for AI interactions, adhering to the principle of data minimization.

6. User Rights and Requests:

Establish mechanisms to fulfill user rights as defined by regulations, such as data access, rectification, erasure, and data portability.

7. Data Security and Protection:

Implement strong security measures to safeguard user data during AI interactions.

Utilize encryption protocols for data in transit and at rest.

Employ access controls and authentication mechanisms to prevent unauthorized access.

8. Vendor Due Diligence:

Assess the data privacy practices of third-party vendors or platforms used for ChatGPT integration.

Review data processing agreements (DPAs) to ensure vendors comply with regulations and protect user data.

Confirm that vendors have appropriate security measures in place to safeguard data.

9. Data Breach Response Plan:

Develop a comprehensive plan to respond to potential data breaches or security incidents promptly and effectively.

10. Regular Audits and Compliance Checks:

Conduct regular audits of data processing activities to ensure ongoing compliance with regulations.

Monitor AI interactions to ensure they align with data protection standards.

Regularly review and update privacy policies and notices to reflect any changes in data processing practices.

11. Training and Awareness:

Educate employees and team members about data privacy regulations, AI usage, and ethical data handling.

12. Appoint a Data Protection Officer (DPO):

If required by regulations, designate a DPO responsible for overseeing data protection activities and compliance.

13. International Data Transfers:

When transferring data across international borders, ensure compliance with regulations related to cross-border data transfers.

By meticulously following these steps, businesses can ensure that ChatGPT integration adheres to data privacy regulations, maintaining the privacy rights and trust of their users while harnessing the benefits of AI technology. Remember that data privacy is an ongoing commitment, and regular updates and improvements are essential to uphold compliance in a rapidly evolving regulatory landscape.

Training and Fine-Tuning

Training and fine-tuning ChatGPT is a pivotal aspect of ensuring that the AI aligns with your business objectives, brand voice, and customer needs. This section delves into the best practices for training and refining ChatGPT to achieve optimal results within your specific business context.

Understanding Fine-Tuning:

Fine-tuning involves customizing the pre-trained ChatGPT model to make it more relevant and aligned with your specific requirements.

1. Define Objectives:

Clearly define your training objectives. Are you enhancing customer support, generating content, or achieving other specific outcomes?

2. Prepare Training Data:

Compile a diverse and representative dataset that includes examples of the type of interactions you want ChatGPT to handle.

3. Annotate Data:

Label your training data to indicate correct responses, desired behavior, and context for different scenarios.

4. Create Prompts:

Develop prompts or instructions that guide the AI's responses in a way that aligns with your brand and objectives.

5. Model Configuration:

Select a base model and configure its parameters for fine-tuning. Adjust settings like temperature and max tokens for response diversity and length.

6. Training Iterations:

Iteratively train the model, evaluating its performance at each stage. Adjust training parameters based on feedback.

User Feedback Loop:

Continuously gather user feedback and adjust the AI model to improve its performance over time.

1. Monitor Interactions:

Regularly review AI-generated interactions to identify errors, inaccuracies, or areas for improvement.

2. Update Training Data:

Incorporate real user interactions into your training dataset to capture real-world scenarios and user preferences.

3. Refine Prompts:

Refine prompts and instructions to guide the AI toward desired responses and enhance its understanding of user intent.

Ethical Considerations:

Maintain ethical standards throughout the training process to ensure that AI-generated content is aligned with your brand values.

1. Avoid Bias:

Monitor and address any biases that may emerge in AI-generated content, striving for fair and inclusive interactions.

2. Human Review:

Include human reviewers in the training process to assess and improve AI responses for quality and appropriateness.

3. Regular Audit:

Periodically audit AI interactions to identify and rectify any deviations from ethical guidelines.

Monitoring Performance:

Use metrics and feedback mechanisms to measure the AI's performance and make informed adjustments.

1. User Satisfaction:

Gather user feedback on AI interactions to gauge satisfaction and identify areas needing improvement.

2. Key Performance Indicators (KPIs):

Define KPIs aligned with your business objectives, such as response accuracy, resolution time, or engagement rates.

By following these training and fine-tuning practices, businesses can ensure that ChatGPT is finely tuned to cater to their specific needs, providing accurate, relevant, and context-aware responses that enhance customer interactions and contribute to business success. As we continue, we will explore additional tools and strategies for leveraging ChatGPT effectively in various business contexts.

Training ChatGPT for Domain-Specific Knowledge

Training ChatGPT to possess domain-specific knowledge is a valuable approach to tailor the AI's responses to your business's unique requirements. This section outlines the steps and considerations for enhancing ChatGPT's expertise in a particular domain.

1. Define the Domain:

Clearly define the specific domain or industry for which you want to train ChatGPT. Whether it's healthcare, finance, technology, or any other field, a well-defined domain is essential.

2. Gather Training Data:

Collect a diverse dataset of text related to the chosen domain. This can include articles, manuals, reports, and other relevant content that covers a range of topics within the domain.

3. Annotate and Label Data:

Annotate the training data by labeling passages that represent accurate and comprehensive information about various topics within the domain.

4. Create Domain-Specific Prompts:

Craft prompts and instructions that reflect the kind of responses you want ChatGPT to generate within the selected domain. These prompts guide the AI's learning process.

5. Adapt Model Configuration:

Adjust the parameters of the ChatGPT model to align with the specific domain. Tweak settings like temperature and max tokens to produce domain-relevant and accurate responses.

6. Iterative Training and Feedback:

Train the model iteratively, evaluating its performance and incorporating user feedback to refine its understanding of the domain.

7. Incorporate User Interactions:

Integrate real user interactions related to the domain into your training dataset. This helps the AI learn from practical scenarios and user preferences.

8. Human Review and Validation:

Involve human reviewers who are knowledgeable in the domain to assess the AI-generated responses for accuracy and relevance.

9. Ethical and Bias Considerations:

Maintain vigilance for potential biases and ethical considerations. Monitor the AI's responses to ensure they are aligned with ethical guidelines and values.

10. Continuous Learning:

Continue to fine-tune the model over time as new information emerges within the domain. Regularly update the training dataset to keep the AI's knowledge up to date.

11. Domain-Specific Knowledge Base:

Build a knowledge base that the AI can reference when generating responses. This repository of accurate information serves as a resource for the AI's learning.

12. Measuring Success:

Define metrics to assess the AI's success in responding to domain-specific inquiries accurately and providing valuable insights.

13. Monitoring and Improvement:

Regularly audit the AI-generated content and interactions to ensure they align with the domain's requirements. Implement improvements based on user feedback and evolving needs.

Training ChatGPT for domain-specific knowledge requires a well-crafted approach that combines domain expertise, curated data, iterative learning, and ethical considerations. By following these steps, businesses can develop a ChatGPT model that enhances customer interactions, provides accurate information, and adds significant value within their chosen domain.

Best Practices for Fine-Tuning the Model

Fine-tuning the ChatGPT model is a nuanced process that requires careful consideration and methodology. This section outlines the best practices to ensure effective fine-tuning and achieve the desired outcomes for your business.

1. Define Clear Objectives:

Clearly define the specific goals and outcomes you aim to achieve through fine-tuning. Whether it's improving response quality, aligning with brand voice, or domain-specific expertise, having well-defined objectives is essential.

2. Curate High-Quality Training Data:

Compile a diverse and representative dataset that encompasses the range of interactions and scenarios you want the AI to handle. High-quality data is crucial for successful fine-tuning.

3. Annotate and Label Data:

Annotate the training data to provide explicit instructions and context for the desired AI responses. Label data instances that exemplify accurate and relevant interactions.

4. Design Effective Prompts:

Craft prompts that guide the AI's responses in a way that aligns with your business objectives, brand identity, and the desired tone of communication.

5. Choose the Right Base Model:

Select a base model that closely matches the type of interactions you're targeting. Different models have varying degrees of context and specificity.

6. Adjust Hyperparameters:

Experiment with hyperparameters such as temperature and max tokens. Temperature controls the randomness of responses, while max tokens limits the length of generated output.

7. Iterative Training:

Fine-tune the model iteratively, evaluating its performance at each stage. Use metrics and user feedback to inform adjustments to training parameters.

8. Incorporate User Feedback:

Incorporate real user interactions into the training dataset to refine the AI's responses based on practical scenarios and user preferences.

9. Human Review and Validation:

Engage human reviewers who understand the context and desired outcomes to assess AI-generated responses for accuracy, relevance, and alignment with objectives.

10. Address Bias and Ethics:

Monitor AI-generated content for biases and ethical considerations. Implement safeguards to ensure that responses are unbiased, fair, and respectful.

11. Regularly Audit Performance:

Conduct regular audits of AI-generated interactions to identify areas for improvement, update training data, and enhance model performance.

12. Monitor Model Drift:

Continuously track the model's performance over time to ensure it maintains alignment with your objectives and doesn't drift away from desired behavior.

13. Use a Test Set:

Maintain a separate test set of data that is not used in training. This set helps you evaluate the model's performance on unseen examples.

14. Measure Success Metrics:

Define success metrics aligned with your objectives, such as response accuracy, user satisfaction, or other relevant KPIs.

15. Regular Retraining and Updates:

AI models evolve, and so should your fine-tuning efforts. Regularly retrain the model to incorporate new data and adjust to changing business needs.

By adhering to these best practices, businesses can fine-tune the ChatGPT model effectively, ensuring that the AI's responses align with their goals, meet user expectations, and contribute positively to their business operations.

4. Applications Across Industries

E-Commerce

The integration of ChatGPT presents transformative opportunities for various industries, and one sector that particularly benefits is e-commerce. This chapter explores how e-commerce businesses can leverage ChatGPT to enhance customer engagement, streamline processes, and create personalized shopping experiences.

Enhancing Customer Engagement:

1. Personalized Product Recommendations:

Utilize ChatGPT to analyze customer preferences, past purchases, and browsing history to provide tailored product recommendations that match individual interests.

2. Virtual Shopping Assistants:

Deploy AI-powered virtual assistants on e-commerce platforms to guide customers through product selection, answer questions, and provide real-time assistance.

3. Interactive Shopping Experience:

Enable customers to interact with ChatGPT to inquire about product details, sizes, availability, and pricing, replicating the in-store shopping experience online.

Streamlining Purchase Process:

1. Order Tracking and Updates:

Integrate ChatGPT to offer automated order tracking and status updates, keeping customers informed about their purchases and delivery.

2. Seamless Checkout Support:

Assist customers with checkout-related queries, address common concerns, and troubleshoot any issues that may arise during the payment process.

3. Return and Refund Assistance:

Provide automated guidance on the return and refund process, helping customers navigate these procedures smoothly.

Personalized Customer Service:

1. Customer Support Anytime, Anywhere:

Deploy ChatGPT-powered chatbots to offer 24/7 customer support, ensuring assistance is available whenever customers need it.

2. Quick Query Resolution:

Address common customer inquiries instantly, allowing human agents to focus on complex issues that require a personal touch.

3. Order Modification Assistance:

Help customers modify orders, change shipping addresses, or update preferences through AI-driven interactions.

Creating Interactive Shopping Experiences:

1. Virtual Try-Ons:

Integrate AI-powered solutions that allow customers to virtually try on products like clothing, accessories, or cosmetics, enhancing their decision-making process.

2. Product Information and Reviews:

Offer detailed product information, user reviews, and comparisons through interactive AI interactions, aiding customers in making informed choices.

3. Interactive Shopping Carts:

Enable AI-driven interactions within shopping carts to suggest complementary products, upsell items, or inform customers about ongoing promotions.

By embracing ChatGPT, e-commerce businesses can elevate customer interactions, streamline shopping processes, and deliver highly personalized experiences. As we delve deeper into this chapter, we'll explore how ChatGPT's capabilities extend to other industries, revealing its potential to revolutionize various sectors.

Enhancing User Experience on E-Commerce Platforms

In the world of e-commerce, providing a seamless and engaging user experience is paramount to success. Leveraging ChatGPT can significantly enhance user interactions and create a more personalized and satisfying shopping journey. This section explores various strategies for optimizing user experience on e-commerce platforms using ChatGPT.

1. Personalized Recommendations:

Implement AI-powered recommendation systems that use ChatGPT to understand customer preferences, browsing behavior, and purchase history. Provide tailored product suggestions that resonate with individual interests.

2. Natural Language Search:

Enhance the search functionality on your e-commerce platform with ChatGPT. Allow users to perform natural language searches, making it easier to find products and navigate the catalog.

3. Interactive Product Descriptions:

Utilize ChatGPT to create interactive product descriptions that respond to user queries. Provide detailed information about products, sizes, colors, and specifications in a conversational manner.

4. Virtual Shopping Assistants:

Integrate AI-driven virtual shopping assistants that guide users through the platform, helping them discover products, answer questions, and make purchase decisions.

5. Personalized Shopping Journeys:

Offer users the option to engage with ChatGPT to curate their shopping experience. Provide personalized recommendations, discounts, and promotions based on their preferences.

6. Real-time Customer Support:

Incorporate AI-powered chatbots that offer instant customer support. Assist users with order tracking, product inquiries, and general assistance, enhancing user satisfaction.

7. Interactive Product Demos:

Enable users to interact with ChatGPT-powered demos that showcase product features and functionalities. This immersive experience can aid users in understanding products better.

8. Virtual Try-Ons and Fittings:

Introduce virtual fitting rooms or try-on experiences where users can visualize how products like clothing, accessories, or cosmetics look on them.

9. User-generated Content Interaction:

Allow users to interact with AI to explore user-generated content, reviews, and testimonials, helping them make more informed purchasing decisions.

10. Guided Shopping Tours:

Create AI-guided shopping tours that introduce users to various product categories and help them explore your platform efficiently.

11. Proactive Assistance:

Initiate proactive AI interactions to assist users at critical points in their shopping journey, such as when they've added items to their cart or during the checkout process.

12. Post-Purchase Follow-up:

Utilize ChatGPT to engage with users after their purchase, providing order updates, offering related products, and encouraging feedback.

By weaving ChatGPT-powered interactions into your e-commerce platform, you can elevate user engagement, simplify the shopping process, and foster a more personalized and enjoyable experience. As we delve further into this chapter, we'll explore how ChatGPT's capabilities extend beyond e-commerce, impacting various industries in innovative ways.

Assisting Customers in Product Selection and Purchase Decisions

Empowering customers to make informed product choices and purchase decisions is a cornerstone of successful e-commerce. With ChatGPT, businesses can offer personalized guidance, answer queries, and address concerns, thereby enhancing the overall shopping experience. This section delves into how ChatGPT can assist customers in navigating product selection and purchase decisions.

1. Product Recommendations:

Implement AI-driven recommendation systems that analyze customer preferences, browsing history, and demographics to suggest relevant products tailored to individual tastes.

2. Interactive Product Queries:

Allow users to interact with ChatGPT to ask detailed questions about products, specifications, features, and compatibility, providing instant and accurate responses.

3. Comparative Analysis:

Enable users to compare different products using ChatGPT, highlighting key differences, advantages, and disadvantages to aid decision-making.

4. Customer Reviews and Insights:

Leverage AI to summarize and present customer reviews, ratings, and testimonials, giving users valuable insights into the experiences of others.

5. Personalized Bundles and Offers:

Create personalized product bundles or special offers based on user preferences, using ChatGPT to explain the value and benefits of each package.

6. Virtual Try-Ons and Fittings:

Introduce virtual try-on experiences using AI-powered visuals, allowing users to see how clothing, accessories, or cosmetics look on them before purchasing.

7. Contextualized Recommendations:

Utilize ChatGPT to recommend products based on the user's current context, such as their browsing behavior, previous interactions, and shopping history.

8. Size and Fit Assistance:

Offer guidance on choosing the right size and fit for clothing, footwear, and accessories through interactive conversations with ChatGPT.

9. Overcoming Purchase Hesitations:

Address common purchase hesitations or objections by using AI to provide relevant information, testimonials, and assurances.

10. Customizable Preferences:

Allow users to set preferences for price ranges, brands, or specific features, and have ChatGPT curate product suggestions accordingly.

11. Budget-Friendly Suggestions:

Assist users in finding suitable products within their budget, recommending alternatives or similar options based on their spending limits.

12. Decision Summaries:

After interacting with users, provide a concise summary of the product options discussed, making it easier for them to compare and make a choice.

13. Wishlist and Favorites Management:

Use ChatGPT to help users manage their wishlists and favorite products, reminding them of saved items and offering related suggestions.

By integrating ChatGPT into the product selection and purchase decision process, e-commerce businesses can offer personalized and valuable assistance to customers, leading to more confident and satisfying shopping experiences. As we progress through this chapter, we'll explore how ChatGPT's capabilities extend to other sectors, contributing to innovation and enhanced customer engagement.

Healthcare

Providing Preliminary Medical Information and Guidance

In the healthcare sector, ChatGPT plays a pivotal role in offering preliminary medical information and guidance to users. This chapter delves into how ChatGPT can assist in providing reliable healthcare information, answering queries, and offering guidance for minor health concerns.

1. Symptom Analysis:

Deploy ChatGPT to engage in conversations with users about their symptoms. Provide preliminary analysis based on user inputs, offering possible causes and suggestions for further action.

2. General Health Information:

Offer general information about common medical conditions, treatments, and preventive measures through interactive conversations.

3. Medication and Dosage Information:

Assist users by answering questions about medication names, usage, dosages, potential side effects, and interactions.

4. Lifestyle Recommendations:

Provide personalized advice on maintaining a healthy lifestyle, including tips on diet, exercise, sleep, and stress management.

5. First Aid Guidance:

Offer step-by-step instructions for basic first aid procedures, helping users respond appropriately to minor injuries or accidents.

6. Identifying Red Flags:

Educate users about symptoms that may indicate a need for urgent medical attention, encouraging them to seek professional help when necessary.

7. Follow-up Care Suggestions:

Guide users on post-treatment care, recovery, and any precautions they should take after receiving medical attention.

8. Mental Health Support:

Engage users in conversations about mental health concerns, offering coping strategies, resources, and information about seeking professional help.

9. Appointment Scheduling:

Assist users in scheduling appointments with healthcare providers, offering available time slots and coordinating with medical facilities.

10. Health Tips and News:

Share the latest health tips, news, and updates to keep users informed about wellness trends and developments.

11. Reliable Medical Resources:

Recommend trustworthy medical websites, resources, and organizations where users can access accurate and up-to-date information.

12. Handling Medical Anxiety:

Guide users in managing medical anxiety or uncertainty, providing reassurance and information to alleviate concerns.

13. Data Privacy and Confidentiality:

Emphasize the importance of data privacy and assure users that their health-related information is treated with confidentiality and security.

By integrating ChatGPT into healthcare services, organizations can offer users quick access to preliminary medical information, guidance, and resources, contributing to informed decision-making and empowering individuals to take charge of their health. As we explore further in this chapter, we'll discover how ChatGPT's capabilities extend to revolutionizing diverse industries, including healthcare.

Assisting in Appointment Scheduling and Patient Inquiries

In the healthcare sector, leveraging ChatGPT can significantly streamline appointment scheduling and address patient inquiries, contributing to improved patient experiences. This section delves into how ChatGPT can assist in managing appointments and providing prompt responses to patient queries.

1. Appointment Scheduling:

Implement ChatGPT-powered systems that allow patients to schedule appointments seamlessly. Offer available time slots, specialties, and locations for medical consultations.

2. Appointment Reminders:

Send automated appointment reminders through ChatGPT, ensuring patients receive timely notifications about upcoming medical visits.

3. Rescheduling and Cancellations:

Enable patients to reschedule or cancel appointments by interacting with ChatGPT, simplifying the process and minimizing no-shows.

4. Specialty and Provider Information:

Provide information about medical specialties, available healthcare providers, their expertise, and credentials to help patients make informed choices.

5. Location and Facility Details:

Assist patients in finding healthcare facilities, clinics, or hospitals by offering location details, directions, and contact information.

6. Insurance Verification:

Guide patients through the process of verifying insurance coverage and understanding the insurance-related aspects of their medical visits.

7. Medical Records Access:

Assist patients in accessing their medical records, test results, and reports through secure and guided interactions.

8. Prescription Refills:

Enable patients to request prescription refills through ChatGPT, guiding them through the process and ensuring accurate communication.

9. Patient Queries:

Address common patient inquiries about clinic hours, medical procedures, preparation instructions for tests, and more.

10. Follow-up Appointments:

Offer guidance on scheduling follow-up appointments after medical procedures, ensuring continuity of care.

11. Telehealth Options:

Inform patients about telehealth services, guiding them through the process of scheduling virtual consultations.

12. Feedback and Suggestions:

Allow patients to provide feedback about their experiences and suggest improvements, enhancing the quality of care.

13. Data Privacy Assurance:

Reiterate the commitment to data privacy and confidentiality when handling patient information and inquiries.

By integrating ChatGPT into appointment scheduling and patient inquiries, healthcare institutions can streamline administrative processes, improve patient engagement, and provide efficient and accessible communication channels. As we continue to explore ChatGPT's applications across industries, we'll uncover its potential to innovate various sectors, including healthcare.

Finance

Answering Customer Queries about Banking and Financial Services

In the finance sector, ChatGPT proves invaluable in addressing customer queries about banking, investments, and financial services. This chapter delves into how ChatGPT can assist in providing accurate information, guiding customers, and enhancing their understanding of financial matters.

1. Account Information:

Engage with customers to provide real-time updates on account balances, transactions, and recent activities.

2. Transaction Inquiries:

Assist customers in reviewing and understanding specific transactions, helping them identify and resolve any discrepancies.

3. Online Banking Assistance:

Guide users through online banking platforms, helping them navigate features such as fund transfers, bill payments, and account linking.

4. Product and Service Information:

Offer details about various banking products, such as savings accounts, loans, credit cards, and investment options.

5. Interest Rates and Fees:

Provide information on current interest rates, fees, and charges associated with different financial services.

6. Investment Insights:

Engage customers in discussions about investment options, explaining concepts, risks, and potential returns.

7. Loan Eligibility and Application:

Assist customers in determining their eligibility for loans and guide them through the application process.

8. Financial Planning Basics:

Offer foundational insights into financial planning, budgeting, and saving strategies to help customers make informed decisions.

9. Fraud and Security Concerns:

Educate customers about common fraud risks, security measures, and steps to take in case of suspicious activities.

10. Retirement Planning:

Provide preliminary guidance on retirement planning, explaining retirement accounts, investment vehicles, and long-term strategies.

11. Tax-related Inquiries:

Assist customers with general tax-related queries, such as understanding tax implications, deductions, and filing procedures.

12. Calculators and Tools:

Integrate financial calculators powered by ChatGPT to help customers estimate loan payments, investment returns, and savings goals.

13. Data Privacy Assurance:

Reiterate the commitment to data privacy and security when handling sensitive financial information.

14. Contact Information and Support:

Offer customers avenues to connect with human agents for more complex inquiries, ensuring comprehensive support.

By incorporating ChatGPT into customer interactions, the finance industry can elevate customer service, enhance financial literacy, and provide efficient responses to a wide range of inquiries. As we continue to explore ChatGPT's applications across industries, we'll uncover its potential to innovate various sectors, including finance.

Providing Basic Financial Advice and Account Information

In the world of finance, ChatGPT offers a valuable tool for delivering basic financial advice and assisting customers with their account-related queries. This section delves into how ChatGPT can provide helpful insights, answer questions, and enhance customer understanding of financial matters.

1. Account Balances and Transactions:

Engage with customers to provide up-to-date information on account balances, recent transactions, and account activities.

2. Transaction Clarifications:

Assist customers in understanding specific transactions by explaining the details, categorizing them, and addressing any concerns.

3. Payment and Transfer Assistance:

Guide users through making payments, fund transfers, and bill payments, offering step-by-step instructions.

4. Savings and Investment Guidance:

Offer basic advice on savings strategies, types of investments, and the importance of diversification.

5. Budgeting Tips:

Provide customers with fundamental budgeting tips and advice to help them manage their finances more effectively.

6. Debt Management Insights:

Offer general insights into managing debt, explaining the importance of timely payments and strategies to reduce debt.

7. Interest Rates and Terms:

Explain the concept of interest rates, how they affect loans and savings, and provide information about various financial terms.

8. Retirement Planning Basics:

Engage customers in discussions about retirement planning, highlighting the significance of early planning and investment options.

9. Tax Planning Insights:

Offer introductory information about tax planning, including deductions, credits, and the importance of accurate record-keeping.

10. Online Banking Assistance:

Guide users through online banking features, such as updating personal information, changing passwords, and setting up alerts.

11. Financial Tools and Resources:

Recommend online financial calculators, budgeting apps, and resources that can help customers manage their finances.

12. Data Privacy Assurance:

Emphasize the security measures in place to protect customer data and reinforce the commitment to privacy.

13. Access to Human Support:

Provide information about reaching out to human representatives for more complex inquiries, ensuring comprehensive assistance.

By integrating ChatGPT into financial interactions, institutions can enhance customer engagement, provide valuable financial advice, and assist customers in managing their accounts effectively. As we continue exploring ChatGPT's applications across various industries, we'll uncover its potential to innovate and enhance user experiences.

5. The Role of AI in Business:

Automation and Efficiency

In the modern landscape of business, the integration of AI technologies has emerged as a transformative force, revolutionizing the way organizations operate, strategize, and connect with customers. At the forefront of this transformation lies automation, a cornerstone of AI's contribution to streamlining processes, optimizing operations, and elevating efficiency to unprecedented levels.

Automation, driven by AI-powered solutions like ChatGPT, has ushered in a new era of operational excellence. It enables businesses to delegate repetitive and time-consuming tasks to intelligent machines, freeing up human resources to focus on high-value activities that require creativity, critical thinking, and strategic decision-making. The result? A more agile and responsive business environment that maximizes productivity and innovation.

At the heart of AI-driven automation is the concept of efficiency enhancement. Mundane tasks that were once manual endeavors are now executed seamlessly by AI systems, minimizing errors and reducing the potential for bottlenecks. For instance, customer inquiries and support interactions can be efficiently managed through AI-powered chatbots like ChatGPT, providing instantaneous responses, reducing wait times, and enhancing overall user satisfaction.

The applications of automation extend across various business functions. In e-commerce, AI-driven recommendation systems powered by ChatGPT analyze user preferences and historical data to curate personalized product suggestions, significantly boosting customer engagement and driving sales. In healthcare, the preliminary analysis and guidance offered by AI models can alleviate strain on medical professionals, enabling them to allocate more time to critical patient care.

The implications for financial institutions are equally profound. ChatGPT's ability to provide accurate and informative responses to customer inquiries about banking, investments, and financial services not only enhances customer satisfaction but also accelerates decision-making processes. Moreover, AI's predictive capabilities empower businesses with data-driven insights, enabling them to forecast trends, optimize inventory, and make strategic choices based on real-time information.

However, as organizations embrace AI-driven automation, a balance between efficiency and ethical considerations becomes paramount. Ensuring transparency in AI interactions, addressing biases in AI-generated content, and safeguarding user data are critical components of responsible AI deployment. Ethical AI practices not only uphold trust but also underscore an organization's commitment to responsible innovation.

The integration of AI-powered automation stands as a pivotal driver of efficiency in the business landscape. With its capacity to offload routine tasks, facilitate faster decision-making, and elevate customer interactions, AI technologies like ChatGPT offer businesses the potential to unlock new levels of productivity, creativity, and growth. As we delve deeper into the evolving role of AI in various industries, we will uncover its dynamic impact on reshaping business paradigms and driving sustainable success.

Streamlining Repetitive Tasks through AI Automation

In the rapidly evolving landscape of business, one of the most transformative contributions of AI is its role in streamlining repetitive tasks through automation. This shift has fundamentally altered the way organizations operate, optimizing efficiency and unleashing new possibilities for growth.

Unlocking Operational Efficiency:

AI-driven automation leverages the capabilities of advanced algorithms and machine learning to handle tasks that were once time-consuming and manual. Mundane activities, such as data entry, sorting, and routine customer inquiries, are now seamlessly executed by AI systems like ChatGPT. This liberation from repetitive tasks empowers human resources to engage in higher-value activities that demand creativity, problem-solving, and strategic thinking.

Enhancing User Experiences:

In the world of customer engagement, AI automation has revolutionized interactions. Chatbots powered by technologies like ChatGPT provide instant responses to customer queries, eliminating wait times and enhancing user experiences. Whether it's providing personalized product recommendations in e-commerce or offering preliminary medical information in healthcare, AI-driven solutions ensure that users receive prompt and accurate information.

Accelerating Decision-Making:

Businesses thrive on informed decision-making, and AI automation expedites this process. Data analysis, trend forecasting, and performance evaluations are now more efficient, thanks to AI's ability to process vast amounts of information in real-time. This empowers organizations to make agile and data-driven choices that shape strategies and outcomes.

Precision and Consistency:

Automation eliminates the risk of human error inherent in repetitive tasks. AI systems perform tasks consistently and accurately, ensuring that the quality of work remains high. From financial calculations to inventory management, AI's precision contributes to reliable and error-free operations.

Adapting to Scalability:

As businesses grow and operations expand, AI automation easily adapts to increased demands. Tasks that were once challenging to scale, such as customer support interactions, can now be efficiently managed through AI systems, ensuring seamless user experiences even during periods of high activity.

Ethics and Responsibility:

While the benefits of AI automation are undeniable, ethical considerations are paramount. Ensuring transparency, addressing biases, and safeguarding user data are vital in the responsible deployment of AI. Businesses must align AI systems with ethical standards to maintain trust and uphold integrity.

AI automation stands as a cornerstone of modern business operations. By liberating human resources from repetitive tasks, enhancing user experiences, accelerating decision-making, and ensuring precision, AI technologies like ChatGPT elevate efficiency and innovation. As we explore the broader role of AI in shaping industries, the impact of automation continues to reshape the landscape of business, creating opportunities for growth, sustainability, and enhanced value creation.

Reducing Operational Costs and Human Error

In the world of AI-driven automation, two compelling benefits stand out prominently: the reduction of operational costs and the mitigation of human error. These advantages have transformative implications for businesses across industries, reshaping workflows, improving efficiency, and elevating overall performance.

Operational Cost Reduction:

AI automation holds the promise of substantial cost savings. By delegating routine and repetitive tasks to AI systems, organizations can optimize resource allocation. Tasks that once demanded significant human labor can now be executed by AI algorithms, leading to reduced staffing needs and associated expenses. Whether it's data entry, invoice processing, or customer inquiries, AI's efficiency translates into lower operational costs and enhanced profitability.

Mitigating Human Error:

Human error has long been a concern in various business processes. From data entry mistakes to miscalculations, errors can lead to financial losses, compliance issues, and reputational damage. AI automation presents a solution by performing tasks with a high degree of accuracy and consistency. Machines don't experience fatigue, distractions, or lapses in attention, minimizing the potential for errors that can impact operations and customer experiences.

Enhancing Resource Allocation:

Efficient resource allocation is a strategic imperative for businesses. By automating repetitive tasks, organizations can allocate their human resources to more strategic and value-added activities. Employees can focus on tasks that require critical thinking, problem-solving, and creativity, leading to a more productive and motivated workforce.

Speed and Scalability:

AI automation operates at unprecedented speeds. Tasks that would take humans hours can be completed by AI systems in a fraction of the time. Moreover, as business demands fluctuate, AI systems can easily scale to meet increased workloads without compromising quality or efficiency.

Quality Control and Consistency:

Consistency is critical for maintaining high standards in business processes. AI automation ensures that tasks are performed with uniform accuracy and adherence to predefined rules. This level of consistency improves the overall quality of work and helps organizations maintain their reputation for excellence.

Strategic Decision-Making:

As operational efficiency improves and human errors decrease, organizations can rely on more accurate and reliable data for strategic decision-making. Timely and precise insights enable better-informed choices, driving growth, innovation, and competitive advantage.

Ethical Considerations:

While the benefits of AI automation are clear, organizations must approach implementation with ethical considerations in mind. Ensuring that AI systems are transparent, unbiased, and aligned with ethical guidelines is essential to building and maintaining trust with customers and stakeholders.

In summary, AI-driven automation presents a dual advantage of reducing operational costs while minimizing human error. By optimizing resource allocation, enhancing accuracy, and accelerating processes, organizations stand to achieve operational excellence, improved customer experiences, and the ability to make more informed decisions. As we explore AI's broader role in reshaping industries, the impact of automation continues to redefine the landscape of modern business.

Data Analysis and Insights:

Utilizing AI to Analyze Market Trends and Customer Behavior
In the age of information, data has emerged as a strategic asset for businesses, providing valuable insights into market dynamics and customer preferences. The integration of AI into data analysis processes has revolutionized how organizations harness these insights, enabling them to make informed decisions, predict trends, and tailor their strategies to meet evolving demands.

Leveraging AI-Powered Insights:

AI algorithms, including those like ChatGPT, are adept at processing vast amounts of data quickly and accurately. This ability has transformed data analysis from a time-consuming endeavor into a real-time and highly accurate process. Businesses can now analyze market trends and customer behavior at unprecedented speeds, enabling them to respond promptly to changing dynamics.

Market Trend Analysis:

AI-driven data analysis empowers businesses to identify and comprehend market trends that might otherwise remain hidden. By processing data from multiple sources, including social media, online platforms, and industry reports, AI can uncover patterns, shifts, and emerging market trends. This information equips organizations with the intelligence needed to adapt their strategies and offerings in alignment with consumer preferences.

Customer Behavior Insights:

Understanding customer behavior is a cornerstone of successful business strategies. AI's ability to analyze large datasets enables businesses to gain deeper insights into customer preferences, purchase patterns, and engagement behaviors. This information drives the creation of personalized experiences, targeted marketing campaigns, and the development of products that resonate with customers.

Predictive Analytics:

AI-powered data analysis transcends traditional reporting by offering predictive capabilities. By identifying patterns and correlations in historical data, AI algorithms can forecast future trends, enabling businesses to proactively address challenges and capitalize on opportunities.

Personalized Marketing Strategies:

AI-driven insights enable businesses to craft personalized marketing strategies. By understanding individual customer preferences and behavior, organizations can tailor their marketing messages, offers, and recommendations to create meaningful and relevant interactions.

Risk Mitigation and Decision-Making:

AI analysis doesn't just focus on opportunities; it also helps identify potential risks. Whether assessing supply chain vulnerabilities or evaluating market volatility, AI algorithms provide data-driven insights that inform risk mitigation strategies and support more informed decision-making.

Ethical Data Usage:

While AI analysis offers immense benefits, ethical considerations must guide data usage. Businesses must respect user privacy, ensure data security, and adhere to regulations governing data collection and usage to maintain trust and compliance.

Making Informed Business Decisions Based on AI-Generated Insights

In the contemporary business landscape, the ability to make well-informed decisions is a defining factor in an organization's success. With the advent of AI-driven insights, businesses are equipped with a powerful tool that not only analyzes vast amounts of data but also provides actionable intelligence to guide strategic choices. This section explores how AI-generated insights empower businesses to navigate complexities, seize opportunities, and optimize outcomes.

Data-Driven Decision-Making:

AI-generated insights offer a paradigm shift in decision-making. Instead of relying solely on intuition or historical data, businesses can now base their choices on real-time, data-driven insights. These insights help validate assumptions, dispel biases, and lead to more objective and accurate decisions.

Understanding Market Dynamics:

Market trends can be elusive, evolving rapidly due to various factors. AI-generated insights allow organizations to understand these dynamics by analyzing data from diverse sources. This enables businesses to adapt to changing market conditions, identify emerging trends, and respond strategically to shifts in consumer preferences.

Customer-Centric Strategies:

At the heart of successful businesses lies the ability to cater to customer needs effectively. AI-generated insights delve deep into customer behavior, preferences, and feedback. This understanding enables businesses to craft customer-centric strategies, offer personalized experiences, and develop products that align with consumer desires.

Optimizing Operations:

From supply chain management to resource allocation, AI-generated insights provide a holistic view of business operations. Organizations can identify bottlenecks, streamline processes, and optimize efficiency by leveraging data-driven recommendations.

Risk Management and Mitigation:

Businesses inherently face risks, whether from market volatility, competition, or unforeseen events. AI-generated insights facilitate risk assessment by analyzing historical data and current conditions. This empowers organizations to proactively devise risk mitigation strategies and contingency plans.

Agile Adaptation:

In a rapidly changing business environment, agility is crucial. AI-generated insights enable organizations to pivot quickly and adapt strategies based on real-time data. This responsive approach ensures that businesses stay ahead of trends and capitalize on emerging opportunities.

Innovation and Product Development:

AI-generated insights can guide innovation and product development. By analyzing customer feedback, market trends, and emerging technologies, businesses can identify gaps in the market and design products that address unmet needs.

Future Trends

Exploring the Evolving Landscape of AI in Business

As AI continues its dynamic evolution, the landscape of business is poised for profound transformation. This chapter delves into the future trends that will shape the integration of AI across industries, catalyzing innovation, redefining strategies, and reshaping the very essence of how businesses operate.

Hyper-Personalization:

The future of AI in business revolves around hyper-personalization. AI algorithms will analyze vast datasets to deliver tailored experiences to each individual customer. From product recommendations to marketing messages, businesses will leverage AI to create experiences that resonate on a deeply personal level.

Augmented Decision-Making:

AI will emerge as a critical partner in decision-making processes. By offering insights, generating scenarios, and simulating outcomes, AI will enhance the decision-making capabilities of human leaders. This symbiotic relationship between AI and human decision-makers will lead to more informed, strategic choices.

AI in Creativity:

The perception of AI as solely analytical is evolving. AI-driven tools are beginning to contribute to creative processes, from generating artwork to composing music. Businesses will harness AI's creative potential to ideate, innovate, and push the boundaries of artistic expression.

Human-Machine Collaboration:

The future will witness a harmonious collaboration between humans and AI. Businesses will capitalize on AI's efficiency in handling repetitive tasks, enabling human employees to focus on tasks that require empathy, critical thinking, and complex problem-solving.

AI for Sustainability:

Sustainability will be a driving force behind AI applications. From optimizing energy consumption to reducing waste in supply chains, AI will play a pivotal role in helping businesses achieve their sustainability goals.

Ethical AI:

As AI's influence grows, ethical considerations will take center stage. Businesses will prioritize transparency, fairness, and accountability in AI algorithms. Ethical AI practices will not only build trust but also ensure compliance with regulations and societal expectations.

Redefining Industries:

AI will disrupt traditional industry boundaries. Sectors such as healthcare, finance, and manufacturing will undergo radical transformation as AI-driven innovations reshape processes, services, and products.

AI Democratization:

The democratization of AI tools will empower small and medium-sized enterprises to leverage AI's capabilities. User-friendly AI platforms will enable businesses to integrate AI without extensive technical expertise.

Continuous Learning AI:

AI models will evolve from static systems to continuous learners. This adaptability will allow AI to stay updated with evolving trends, user behaviors, and market dynamics.

The Ethos of Innovation:

The future landscape will be defined by an ethos of innovation, with AI acting as a catalyst. Businesses that embrace AI-driven innovation will be better equipped to navigate disruptions, seize opportunities, and lead in their respective industries.

The future trends of AI in business hold promise for a world where personalization, collaboration, and sustainability converge. As AI becomes an integral part of the business fabric, organizations that adeptly embrace these trends will position themselves at the forefront of innovation, setting the stage for a dynamic and transformative era of business growth and prosperity.

Predictions for How AI Will Continue to Shape Various Industries

The influence of AI on industries is poised to evolve in unprecedented ways, fundamentally reshaping the way businesses operate, interact, and innovate. This section explores predictions for how AI will continue to shape various sectors, paving the way for new paradigms and opportunities.

Healthcare:

AI's impact on healthcare will continue to expand, with predictive analytics playing a crucial role in early disease detection and personalized treatment plans. AI-driven diagnostic tools will enhance accuracy, and telehealth will become more sophisticated, providing remote consultations and reducing healthcare disparities.

Finance:

In finance, AI-powered robo-advisors will gain prominence, providing personalized investment advice and managing portfolios. Fraud detection will become more sophisticated, leveraging AI's ability to analyze patterns and anomalies. Smart contracts based on blockchain and AI will streamline transaction processes and reduce administrative overhead.

Manufacturing:

Manufacturing will see increased automation with AI-driven robotics, optimizing production lines for efficiency and flexibility. Predictive maintenance powered by AI will minimize downtime and maintenance costs. Supply chain management will become more resilient through AI's ability to predict disruptions and adjust logistics in real time.

Retail:

AI will revolutionize the retail experience with hyper-personalization, leveraging data to tailor product recommendations and marketing messages. Augmented reality (AR) and virtual reality (VR) will enhance the in-store and online shopping experience, allowing customers to "try before they buy."

Education:

AI will transform education by enabling personalized learning experiences. Adaptive learning platforms will analyze student progress and tailor educational content to individual needs. AI-driven chatbots will provide instant tutoring and support, enhancing student engagement and outcomes.

Energy:

AI will play a pivotal role in energy management and sustainability. Smart grids will optimize energy distribution, while AI-powered sensors will enhance energy efficiency in buildings. Predictive maintenance of renewable energy infrastructure will ensure optimal performance and reduced downtime.

Transportation:

Autonomous vehicles will continue to advance, with AI-powered systems enhancing safety and efficiency. AI algorithms will optimize traffic flow, reducing congestion and emissions. Drone deliveries and smart traffic management will become more prevalent.

Entertainment:

AI will revolutionize content creation in the entertainment industry. AI-generated music, art, and literature will become more sophisticated. Content recommendation algorithms will further personalize entertainment experiences, leading to immersive and engaging interactions.

Agriculture:

Precision agriculture will thrive with AI-driven insights. Drones and sensors will monitor crop health, optimize irrigation, and enhance yields. AI-powered predictive analytics will assist in disease prevention and yield forecasting.

Construction:

AI will streamline construction processes, optimizing project timelines and budgets. AI-powered design tools will enhance architectural and engineering tasks. Construction site safety will improve through AI-driven monitoring and predictive risk assessment.

The transformative potential of AI is vast and multifaceted. As industries continue to embrace AI's capabilities, innovation will flourish, operations will be optimized, and user experiences will be elevated to unprecedented levels. Businesses that adapt to these AI-driven changes will be well-positioned to thrive in a rapidly evolving landscape.

6. Generating Revenue with ChatGPT

In the world of business, revenue generation is a fundamental goal. The integration of AI, specifically ChatGPT, offers innovative avenues to drive revenue, enhance customer engagement, and create new monetization strategies. This chapter delves into how organizations can harness the power of ChatGPT to unlock revenue streams, foster customer loyalty, and maximize the value of AI-driven interactions.

Elevating Customer Engagement:

Customer engagement lies at the heart of revenue generation. ChatGPT's ability to provide instant, personalized interactions with customers leads to heightened engagement. By offering real-time responses, addressing inquiries, and facilitating seamless interactions, businesses can forge stronger connections with their audience, fostering brand loyalty and repeat business.

Enhancing User Experiences:

AI-powered interactions with ChatGPT elevate user experiences, making interactions more efficient, informative, and enjoyable. Enhanced user experiences contribute to positive brand perception, encouraging customers to engage more deeply and frequently with businesses, ultimately leading to increased revenue opportunities.

Personalized Recommendations:

ChatGPT's capacity to analyze user preferences and behaviors enables businesses to provide personalized product recommendations. By understanding customer needs and suggesting relevant offerings, businesses can drive cross-selling and upselling, increasing the average transaction value and overall revenue.

Expanding Market Reach:

Language barriers can limit market reach, but ChatGPT can bridge this gap by providing multi-language support. Businesses can engage with a global audience, expanding their reach and tapping into new markets that were previously untapped, ultimately resulting in diversified revenue streams.

Monetizing Premium Services:

ChatGPT's advanced capabilities can be monetized through premium services. Offering premium subscription plans that provide enhanced features, faster response times, or access to specialized content can generate a steady stream of recurring revenue.

AI-Powered E-Commerce:

In the e-commerce landscape, ChatGPT can function as a virtual shopping assistant, guiding customers through product selection, answering queries, and even assisting in completing purchases. This seamless shopping experience enhances conversion rates and drives e-commerce revenue.

Data-Driven Marketing:

ChatGPT's interactions generate valuable user data that can be leveraged for targeted marketing campaigns. By analyzing user interactions and preferences, businesses can design more effective marketing strategies that resonate with customers, resulting in higher conversion rates and increased revenue.

Customer Support Monetization:

Efficient customer support powered by ChatGPT can be offered as a value-added service to other businesses. Providing AI-driven customer support solutions can create a new revenue stream and position organizations as leaders in customer service innovation.

Innovative Revenue Models:

ChatGPT enables businesses to explore innovative revenue models. From pay-per-use AI interactions to AI-generated content subscriptions, organizations can craft unique offerings that cater to specific customer needs, unlocking revenue potential.

Balancing Monetization and User Experience:

While revenue generation is a goal, maintaining a positive user experience is paramount. Striking a balance between monetization efforts and providing genuine value to customers is essential to avoid alienating users and preserving brand trust.

ChatGPT presents a versatile tool for generating revenue by fostering customer engagement, personalizing experiences, and unlocking innovative monetization strategies. By strategically integrating ChatGPT into business operations, organizations can enhance their revenue potential, while simultaneously delivering enhanced value to customers. As we delve deeper into the evolving role of AI in business, revenue generation stands as a testament to the transformative power of AI-driven interactions.

Subscription Models

Offering Premium Access to Enhanced AI Interactions

Subscription models are a proven strategy to generate recurring revenue while providing enhanced value to customers. Leveraging AI interactions, such as ChatGPT, for subscription-based services can unlock new revenue streams and foster deeper customer engagement.

Businesses can offer premium subscribers access to AI interactions with advanced capabilities. This could include faster response times, more accurate recommendations, or extended conversation lengths. By providing these enhanced features, businesses can entice customers to subscribe for a higher level of service.

Premium subscriptions can provide personalized experiences that cater to individual preferences and needs. AI-powered interactions can analyze user behavior and adjust responses accordingly, ensuring that subscribers receive relevant and meaningful interactions.

Subscribers can gain access to exclusive AI-generated content, such as in-depth reports, analyses, or specialized insights. This content can be curated to cater to subscribers' interests, establishing a sense of exclusivity and value.

Premium subscribers can enjoy priority customer support powered by AI. This means quicker response times and more comprehensive assistance, enhancing the overall customer experience.

Creating subscription tiers with varying features allows businesses to cater to a broader range of customer needs and preferences. By offering different levels of service, businesses can capture diverse segments of their audience and generate revenue accordingly.

Businesses can create subscription tiers with escalating features. A basic tier might offer essential AI interactions, while a pro tier could include enhanced personalization and priority support. A premium tier can grant access to all features, including exclusive content and advanced capabilities.

Allowing subscribers to customize their subscription by selecting the features they value most can increase the attractiveness of subscription offerings. This empowers customers to create a subscription plan that aligns with their needs and budget.

Businesses can offer a free tier with limited features to attract users and showcase the value of their AI interactions. Premium subscription tiers can then provide more advanced features and content, encouraging users to upgrade for a more comprehensive experience.

Effectively communicate the value of each subscription tier. Clearly outline the features and benefits of each level, showcasing how each tier addresses different customer needs and adds value.

Offering trial periods for premium subscription tiers can entice users to experience the enhanced features. Additionally, businesses can provide easy options for subscribers to upgrade their plan based on their experience and requirements.

While offering subscription tiers, maintaining a positive user experience is essential. Ensure that even the basic tier offers value and delivers a seamless AI interaction.

Subscription models powered by AI interactions offer a dynamic way to generate revenue while delivering enhanced value to customers. By tailoring features, personalizing experiences, and communicating the value proposition effectively, businesses can foster customer loyalty, engagement, and sustainable revenue growth. As the business landscape evolves, subscription models powered by AI interactions stand as a testament to innovation in monetization strategies.

Creating Subscription Tiers with Varying Features

Subscription models have emerged as a strategic approach that offers ongoing value to customers while ensuring a consistent revenue stream for businesses. Creating subscription tiers with varying features is a dynamic strategy that not only caters to diverse customer needs but also maximizes revenue potential. This section explores the nuances of this approach and how businesses can effectively implement it.

Segmenting Customer Needs:

The foundation of creating subscription tiers lies in understanding the diverse needs of your customer base. By segmenting customers based on their preferences, usage patterns, and requirements, businesses can design subscription tiers that cater to specific demographics or use cases.

Tailoring Features to Tiers:

Each subscription tier should offer a distinct set of features that align with the identified customer segments. For instance, a basic tier might provide essential AI interactions, while higher tiers can introduce advanced capabilities, personalized experiences, or exclusive content.

Gradual Feature Progression:

The subscription tiers should be designed to provide a sense of progression. Moving from one tier to another should feel like an upgrade, with each tier offering a compelling reason to subscribe at that level.

Communicating Value:

Effectively communicating the value of each subscription tier is essential. Clearly articulate the benefits that subscribers will gain with each upgrade. Use concise and engaging language to showcase the enhanced features and experiences available in higher tiers.

Price Differentiation:

Subscription tiers should be priced according to the value they offer. Higher-tier subscriptions with more advanced features can be priced at a premium, reflecting the added benefits subscribers will receive.

Personalization Options:

Consider offering personalization options within subscription tiers. Allowing subscribers to customize their plan by selecting the features most relevant to them enhances the perception of value and caters to individual preferences.

Trial Periods and Upgrades:

To encourage users to explore higher subscription tiers, provide trial periods where they can experience the enhanced features firsthand. Make it easy for subscribers to upgrade their plans, providing a seamless transition from one tier to another.

Retention and Renewals:

Ensuring customer satisfaction is crucial for subscription models. Continuously deliver the promised value and periodically assess customer feedback to refine and enhance subscription offerings.

Monitoring and Adjustments:

Regularly monitor the performance of different subscription tiers. Analyze subscriber engagement, satisfaction, and churn rates to make informed adjustments and refinements to your offerings.

Ethical Considerations:

Maintain transparency and ensure that the features offered in each subscription tier align with customer expectations. Avoid creating artificial limitations or withholding essential features to drive subscribers toward higher tiers.

Creating subscription tiers with varying features is a strategic approach that not only enhances revenue potential but also caters to diverse customer needs. By segmenting customer preferences, tailoring features, and effectively communicating value, businesses can craft subscription models that foster customer loyalty, satisfaction, and sustainable growth. As we explore innovative revenue strategies, subscription tiers stand as a testament to the power of customization and value delivery in the modern business landscape.

Dynamic Value Scaling:

The concept of creating subscription tiers with varying features aligns with the principle of dynamic value scaling. Instead of a one-size-fits-all approach, businesses recognize that different customers have distinct needs. This strategy ensures that customers pay for the value they receive, enhancing their overall satisfaction.

Inclusive Basic Tier:

The basic subscription tier serves as the entry point, providing essential features at an affordable price. This tier aims to include enough value to cater to a wide audience, ensuring that even customers with minimal needs can benefit from the service.

Unveiling Premium Benefits:

As customers explore higher subscription tiers, they unveil premium benefits that enhance their experience. These benefits might include faster response times, access to exclusive content, or advanced AI capabilities. The progressive nature of benefits encourages customers to upgrade for a more comprehensive solution.

Catering to Diverse Preferences:

In the dynamic landscape of customer preferences, catering to various needs is essential. By offering different subscription tiers, businesses ensure that they can address a broader spectrum of customer requirements. This flexibility fosters customer loyalty and reduces the likelihood of churn due to unmet needs.

Strategic Upselling:

Creating subscription tiers provides a structured approach to upselling. Businesses can strategically position the benefits of higher tiers, enticing customers to consider upgrading to access additional features that align with their evolving needs.

Aligning with Customer Growth:

Customers' needs evolve over time, and their subscription can evolve with them. The tiered approach enables businesses to align with customer growth. As customers seek more value, they can seamlessly transition to higher tiers without disruptions.

Value-Driven Expansion:

As businesses expand their offerings, they can introduce new subscription tiers that offer innovative and specialized features. This expansion not only keeps existing customers engaged but also attracts new customers seeking unique solutions.

Monitoring and Flexibility:

The success of subscription tiers relies on continuous monitoring and adaptability. Analyze customer feedback, engagement patterns, and market trends to fine-tune and adjust subscription tiers over time.

Enhancing Customer Satisfaction:

By providing subscription tiers with varying features, businesses actively enhance customer satisfaction. Customers feel that their needs are understood and valued, resulting in a higher perception of the overall service's worth.

Strategic Differentiation:

Subscription tiers differentiate businesses from competitors. They showcase a commitment to providing tailored solutions, elevating the brand as a customer-centric entity that prioritizes individual needs.

The strategy of creating subscription tiers with varying features aligns with the dynamic nature of customer preferences and needs. By offering value that scales according to individual requirements, businesses can foster customer loyalty, drive revenue growth, and establish a brand identity centered around customization and value delivery. As the business landscape evolves, subscription tiers remain a testament to the adaptability and strategic innovation that define successful revenue models.

Consulting and Expertise

Providing AI-Powered Consultation Services to Clients

In the world of business, knowledge and expertise are invaluable assets. The integration of AI, such as ChatGPT, offers organizations an innovative way to provide consultation services to clients. This section explores how businesses can leverage AI-powered consultation to create new revenue streams while delivering informed insights and guidance to clients.

Enhancing Consulting Efficiency:

AI-powered consultation services amplify the efficiency of consulting engagements. ChatGPT can quickly analyze client inquiries, industry trends, and relevant data to provide comprehensive insights in real time. This not only accelerates the consulting process but also ensures that clients receive timely and accurate information.

Scale and Accessibility:

Traditional consulting can be constrained by factors like time zones and availability. AI-powered consultation transcends these limitations, offering clients 24/7 access to expertise. Clients can receive guidance and information whenever they need it, enhancing convenience and accessibility.

Personalized Recommendations:

ChatGPT's ability to analyze client preferences and needs enables personalized recommendations. Whether clients seek business strategies, investment insights, or operational improvements, AI-powered consultation can tailor advice to individual requirements, fostering a stronger client-business relationship.

Data-Driven Insights:

AI-powered consultation relies on data analysis to generate insights. By processing large datasets and identifying patterns, businesses can offer clients data-driven recommendations that enrich decision-making processes.

Scalable Expertise:

AI-powered consultation extends the reach of expertise. Businesses can offer consultation across various domains and industries without limitations tied to the availability of individual experts. This scalability enables organizations to address diverse client needs effectively.

Cost-Effective Solutions:

AI-powered consultation offers cost-effective solutions for clients. Traditional consulting often incurs substantial fees, but AI-powered alternatives can provide valuable insights at a fraction of the cost, democratizing access to expertise.

Monetizing Specialized Knowledge and Assistance

Monetizing specialized knowledge and assistance is a strategic avenue for revenue generation. By offering premium access to AI-powered expertise, businesses can create unique revenue streams while ensuring clients receive specialized guidance.

Premium Subscription Models:

Businesses can offer subscription models that grant clients exclusive access to AI-generated insights and advice. These premium subscriptions can cater to specific industries, niches, or topics, allowing clients to tap into specialized knowledge on an ongoing basis.

Customized Consultation Packages:

AI-powered consultation can be packaged into tailored solutions for clients. By understanding individual needs, businesses can offer consultation packages that provide targeted advice and solutions, catering to unique requirements.

Value-Added Services:

AI-generated insights can be bundled with existing services to create enhanced value for clients. For example, a financial advisory firm could offer AI-generated investment recommendations as an add-on to their traditional services.

Expertise Marketplaces:

Businesses can create marketplaces where clients can access AI-generated expertise on-demand. Clients can choose from a range of topics and receive insights from AI models tailored to their needs.

Transparency and Trust:

Monetization of specialized knowledge must be founded on transparency and trust. Businesses should clearly communicate that AI is assisting in consultation and highlight the benefits of AI-generated insights.

AI-powered consultation services represent a strategic revenue generation opportunity. By leveraging ChatGPT to provide timely, personalized, and data-driven insights, businesses can not only enhance their revenue streams but also deliver value to clients in a new and innovative way. As AI continues to redefine the boundaries of business operations, monetizing expertise through AI-driven consultation emerges as a powerful avenue for growth and client engagement.

Partnerships and Integration

Collaborating with Other Businesses to Integrate AI Solutions

Collaboration is a cornerstone of innovation, and in the context of AI, partnerships offer unique avenues for revenue generation. By collaborating with other businesses to integrate AI solutions, organizations can tap into new markets, enhance their offerings, and create mutually beneficial relationships.

AI Integration Synergies:

Collaborating with businesses that offer complementary products or services can lead to powerful AI integration synergies. For instance, a software company and an AI provider can join forces to enhance the functionality and intelligence of their products.

Market Expansion:

Partnerships allow businesses to expand their market reach. By integrating AI solutions into their partner's offerings, companies can enter new markets and cater to diverse customer needs, ultimately leading to increased revenue opportunities.

Enhancing Offerings:

AI integration can enhance the value of products and services. Businesses can provide clients with innovative features and capabilities powered by AI, setting themselves apart from competitors and justifying premium pricing.

Speed to Market:

Collaborating with an AI provider can expedite the development process. Rather than investing resources to build AI capabilities from scratch, businesses can integrate existing AI solutions, accelerating time-to-market for new offerings.

Shared Resources:

Partnerships enable businesses to pool resources for AI integration efforts. From technical expertise to data resources, collaboration can lead to more efficient and cost-effective AI implementation.

Exploring Revenue-Sharing Models through Partnerships

Partnerships can extend beyond technological integration to revenue-sharing models that create win-win scenarios for businesses. Exploring revenue-sharing models through partnerships can lead to innovative ways of generating revenue and fostering mutually beneficial relationships.

Subscription-Based Sharing:

Businesses can offer joint subscription plans that include both partners' products or services. Revenue generated from the subscriptions can be shared based on agreed-upon terms, creating a continuous revenue stream.

Transaction-Based Sharing:

Partnerships can involve transaction-based sharing models. For instance, an e-commerce platform and an AI recommendation engine could share a portion of the revenue generated from purchases driven by AI-generated recommendations.

Referral Programs:

Businesses can refer clients to their partner's AI solutions and receive a percentage of the revenue generated from those referrals. This encourages cross-promotion and benefits both parties.

Usage-Based Sharing:

In cases where AI usage drives value, partners can establish a usage-based revenue-sharing model. Revenue distribution could be tied to the volume of AI interactions or the benefits derived from AI-driven insights.

Performance-Driven Sharing:

Partnerships can align revenue sharing with performance metrics. If AI integration leads to specific outcomes, such as increased customer engagement or conversion rates, revenue distribution can be tied to these achievements.

Ethical Considerations:

While revenue-sharing partnerships offer lucrative possibilities, ethical considerations are crucial. Partnerships should be transparent, equitable, and aligned with the best interests of all parties involved.

Partnerships and AI integration offer dynamic pathways for revenue generation. By collaborating to integrate AI solutions and exploring innovative revenue-sharing models, businesses can tap into new revenue streams, enhance their market presence, and create value for both themselves and their partners. As AI continues to reshape industries, strategic partnerships become key drivers of sustainable growth and innovation.

7. Overcoming Challenges and Future Developments

The integration of AI, including ChatGPT, into business operations presents a landscape rich with opportunities, but not without its fair share of challenges. This chapter delves into the complexities businesses may encounter and explores the ways in which they can overcome limitations to unlock AI's full potential.

Handling Limitations

Data Quality and Quantity:

A fundamental challenge in AI integration is the quality and quantity of data available. AI models, like ChatGPT, rely on vast datasets for training and fine-tuning. Businesses must ensure that their data is accurate, diverse, and representative of the target audience to prevent biases and errors from affecting AI-generated outcomes.

Bias and Fairness:

AI models can inadvertently inherit biases present in training data. This can lead to AI-generated content that reflects stereotypes or discriminates against certain groups. Businesses must actively address bias through careful data curation, algorithmic fairness measures, and continuous monitoring to ensure ethical AI outputs.

Complex Queries and Context:

AI, while powerful, may struggle with understanding complex queries or maintaining context over extended interactions. Businesses must manage user expectations and design interactions that guide users to provide clearer input when needed, enhancing AI's ability to deliver accurate responses.

Data Privacy and Security:

The integration of AI requires handling sensitive user data. Ensuring data privacy and security is paramount to maintain user trust. Businesses must implement robust data protection measures, adhere to relevant regulations, and adopt encryption techniques to safeguard user information.

Technical Expertise:

Implementing and fine-tuning AI models demands technical expertise. Businesses without in-house AI knowledge may face challenges in setting up and maintaining AI systems. Collaborating with AI experts, hiring skilled professionals, or leveraging user-friendly AI platforms can help overcome this limitation.

Scalability:

As businesses grow, the demand for AI-driven interactions may increase. Ensuring AI systems can scale seamlessly to handle higher user volumes while maintaining performance and response quality is crucial for consistent user experiences.

Future Developments

While challenges exist, the future of AI in business holds promising developments that will reshape industries and augment capabilities.

Advancements in AI Models:

Future AI models will likely exhibit enhanced language understanding, context retention, and even emotional intelligence. These advancements will enable more sophisticated and accurate AI-generated interactions.

Ethical AI Standards:

The industry's focus on ethical AI will intensify. Businesses will work toward establishing standards and guidelines to ensure responsible AI usage, transparency, and accountability.

Human-AI Collaboration:

AI's role will evolve from standalone solutions to collaborative partners. Human-AI collaboration will become more seamless, augmenting human capabilities and decision-making processes.

Customization and Personalization:

AI will offer deeper levels of customization and personalization. Businesses will fine-tune AI models to align with their unique brand voice and cater to specific customer preferences.

Regulatory Landscape:

Regulations surrounding AI usage will continue to evolve. Businesses must stay informed about legal and ethical requirements to ensure compliance and minimize risks.

The journey of integrating AI into business operations is marked by challenges and opportunities. By addressing limitations and staying attuned to future developments, businesses can harness AI's transformative potential to enhance customer experiences, drive revenue, and navigate an ever-evolving landscape. As AI continues to mature and shape industries, the pursuit of innovation and responsible AI deployment will pave the way for a future where businesses thrive in harmony with AI-powered technologies.

Addressing Potential Shortcomings of AI-Generated Content

While AI-generated content offers remarkable capabilities, it's essential to acknowledge and address potential shortcomings to maintain high-quality interactions and user satisfaction.

Content Accuracy and Misinterpretation:

AI models like ChatGPT may generate content that is factually incorrect or misinterprets user queries. To mitigate this, businesses should implement context validation mechanisms, provide clear guidelines to users, and have human oversight to rectify inaccuracies.

Lack of Emotional Understanding:

AI may struggle to comprehend and respond to emotions conveyed by users accurately. Businesses can address this by setting user expectations about the AI's capabilities and by offering human escalation options for emotionally sensitive queries.

Limited Context Retention:

AI models might struggle to maintain context over extended conversations. Implementing strategies like providing conversational history to the AI or guiding users to provide relevant context can help overcome this limitation.

Bias and Offensive Content:

AI-generated content can unintentionally exhibit biases or produce offensive language. Implementing rigorous content moderation processes, regular bias checks, and user reporting mechanisms can help curb the dissemination of biased or inappropriate content.

Strategies for Managing Customer Expectations

Managing customer expectations is key to ensuring a positive user experience and avoiding potential disappointment due to AI limitations.

Transparency about AI Usage:

Clearly communicating that users are interacting with an AI-powered system sets the right expectations. Businesses can provide disclaimers and information about the AI's capabilities, ensuring users understand the nature of the interaction.

Setting Realistic Boundaries:

Clearly defining the scope of AI's abilities helps users understand what tasks AI can handle and what requires human intervention. Businesses should guide users to provide clear and specific queries that align with AI's capabilities.

Offering Human Assistance:

Incorporating an option for users to escalate to human assistance when AI reaches its limits reassures users that their inquiries will be addressed effectively, even if the AI cannot provide a satisfactory answer.

Continuous Learning and Iteration:

Businesses should iterate and improve AI models based on user interactions and feedback. Letting users know that the AI is constantly learning and evolving demonstrates a commitment to enhancing their experience.

Feedback Loops:

Providing users with the ability to provide feedback on AI-generated interactions can help businesses identify areas of improvement and address user concerns promptly.

User Education:

Educating users about best practices for interacting with AI, such as using clear language and providing context, empowers them to extract the most value from AI interactions.

Human-AI Hybrid Solutions:

Promoting the collaboration between AI and human agents can manage expectations effectively. Clearly articulating when a query requires human intervention creates a seamless transition and avoids user frustration.

Balancing AI-generated content's capabilities with user expectations is crucial to ensure positive interactions and foster trust. By acknowledging limitations, setting clear boundaries, and providing avenues for human assistance, businesses can effectively manage user expectations and offer a rewarding AI-powered experience. As AI continues to advance, maintaining transparency and user-centric strategies will be pivotal in delivering exceptional user satisfaction.

Effectively managing customer expectations in the world of AI-generated content is a cornerstone of delivering a positive and satisfying user experience. By implementing thoughtful strategies, businesses can navigate the nuances of AI capabilities while ensuring that users have a clear understanding of what to anticipate.

Transparency and Clear Communication:

At the heart of managing customer expectations lies transparency. Businesses should openly communicate that users are engaging with an AI-powered system. Clear disclaimers and explanations about the AI's role set the stage for a transparent interaction.

Education and Guidelines:

Empowering users with guidelines on how to interact with the AI can enhance their experience. Educating users on best practices, such as providing specific queries and context, helps them utilize the AI effectively and align their expectations with its capabilities.

Scope Definition:

Defining the scope of AI's abilities is vital. Businesses should clearly outline what tasks the AI can handle and what requires human intervention. This clarity helps users avoid frustration and empowers them to make informed choices.

Realistic Responses:

Businesses should ensure that AI-generated responses are accurate and realistic. This prevents users from forming unrealistic expectations and fosters trust in the AI's capabilities.

Human Escalation Path:

Incorporating an option for users to escalate to human assistance when the AI encounters challenges reinforces the commitment to providing effective solutions. This safety net assures users that their inquiries will be resolved, even if the AI isn't equipped to handle them.

Continuous Improvement:

Highlighting the AI's continuous learning and improvement journey reassures users that their feedback matters. Businesses can convey that user interactions contribute to enhancing the AI's performance over time.

Setting Response Time Expectations:

Informing users about the typical response time of the AI manages their expectations regarding the immediacy of interactions. This prevents users from expecting instant responses for complex queries.

Personalization and Customization Limits:

Clearly communicating the extent to which the AI can provide personalized or customized responses helps users understand the AI's limitations. This avoids disappointment if the AI cannot fulfill intricate personalization requests.

User Feedback Channels:

Establishing channels for users to provide feedback on AI interactions invites them to contribute to the AI's refinement. This engagement reinforces a collaborative approach and shows that their input is valued.

Consistency in Tone and Style:

Maintaining a consistent tone and style in AI-generated content fosters familiarity for users. When the AI's responses align with their expectations, users are more likely to engage positively.

Strategies for managing customer expectations in the context of AI-generated content form the bedrock of a successful user experience. By cultivating transparency, offering human support when needed, and continuously improving AI capabilities, businesses can foster trust, deliver value, and ensure that user interactions with AI remain positive and aligned with their expectations. As AI technology evolves, customer-centric strategies will play an instrumental role in optimizing user satisfaction and forging enduring relationships.

Continuous Learning

The Importance of Staying Updated with AI Advancements

In the rapidly evolving landscape of AI, staying updated with the latest advancements is not just beneficial—it's imperative for businesses aiming to maximize the potential of AI integration. The world of AI, including tools like ChatGPT, is marked by constant innovation, and failing to keep pace can lead to missed opportunities, outdated strategies, and a competitive disadvantage.

The significance of continuous learning in AI extends beyond mere technological trends. Understanding new breakthroughs, algorithms, and methodologies enables businesses to harness AI's cutting-edge capabilities. Regularly updated knowledge ensures that businesses are aware of improved performance, enhanced user experiences, and refined functionalities that emerge as AI evolves.

AI's potential to revolutionize operations, drive revenue, and create value underscores the need for businesses to prioritize ongoing education. From improved customer interactions to data-driven insights, businesses that stay informed about AI advancements can effectively adapt their strategies, ensuring they remain agile and prepared for the demands of a dynamic market.

In the dynamic landscape of AI, continuous learning isn't just a recommendation; it's a strategic imperative. The evolution of AI technologies, including ChatGPT, is relentless, and businesses that fail to keep pace risk being left behind. This section emphasizes the significance of staying updated with AI advancements and explores how businesses can leverage ongoing learning to drive innovation, maintain competitiveness, and ensure optimal AI integration.

Dynamic Nature of AI:

AI technologies, driven by rapid advancements and breakthroughs, are in a state of constant evolution. What is groundbreaking today might become standard tomorrow. Staying updated with the latest developments is essential to harnessing AI's full potential.

Competitive Edge:

Businesses that stay current with AI advancements gain a competitive edge. The ability to leverage cutting-edge AI capabilities, such as enhanced language understanding, improved context retention, and refined content generation, positions organizations as leaders in innovation.

Optimizing AI Integration:

As AI technologies advance, new features and functionalities emerge. Staying informed about these advancements enables businesses to optimize their AI integration strategies. They can align AI capabilities with their goals, fine-tune models for specific purposes, and provide users with the latest AI-driven experiences.

Strategic Decision-Making:

Staying updated with AI developments empowers businesses to make strategic decisions informed by the latest trends and insights. Whether it's selecting the right AI platform, determining investment priorities, or identifying emerging opportunities, staying informed ensures decisions are forward-looking and aligned with industry trends.

Adapting to User Expectations:

User expectations evolve alongside AI advancements. Users anticipate AI interactions that are seamless, accurate, and aligned with the state-of-the-art AI capabilities. Businesses that keep up with these advancements can meet and exceed user expectations, driving user satisfaction and loyalty.

Fostering Innovation:

AI advancements often open doors to innovative possibilities. By staying updated, businesses can explore novel use cases, experiment with emerging AI functionalities, and pioneer new ways to leverage AI for revenue generation, customer engagement, and process optimization.

Collaboration and Networking:

Staying connected to AI communities, attending conferences, and engaging in industry discussions fosters collaboration and networking. These interactions provide insights into best practices, success stories, and challenges faced by other businesses, helping organizations navigate their AI journey effectively.

The importance of staying updated with AI advancements cannot be overstated. In a landscape where AI technologies are rewriting possibilities at an unprecedented pace, businesses that commit to continuous learning position themselves as agile, innovative, and responsive entities. By embracing ongoing learning, organizations not only remain at the forefront of AI integration but also lay the foundation for sustainable growth, differentiation, and success in a future shaped by AI-driven possibilities.

Incorporating New Features and Capabilities into Business Strategies

Embracing AI's continuous evolution requires more than just awareness—it demands strategic integration of new features and capabilities into business operations. As AI models like ChatGPT introduce enhanced language understanding, context retention, and other advanced functionalities, businesses that swiftly incorporate these improvements can gain a competitive edge.

Integrating new features involves a strategic assessment of how they align with business goals. For instance, if AI gains the ability to process more complex queries, businesses can explore how to leverage this enhancement to provide deeper insights to customers or streamline complex decision-making processes.

Businesses must be agile in their approach, adapting their strategies to accommodate AI advancements. This might involve revisiting existing use cases, exploring novel applications, and even envisioning entirely new revenue streams that emerge as AI capabilities evolve.

Moreover, incorporating new features necessitates collaboration between technical teams and business stakeholders. This partnership ensures that technical capabilities are aligned with strategic objectives, leading to meaningful and impactful AI integration.

Continuous learning about AI advancements is pivotal for businesses seeking to remain competitive and innovative. By staying informed about the latest breakthroughs and strategically incorporating new features into their operations, businesses can unlock AI's full potential, driving value, efficiency, and growth. As AI continues its transformative journey, businesses that embrace a culture of ongoing learning and strategic integration will be best positioned to thrive in a rapidly changing landscape.

Ethical Evolution:

Navigating Ethical Challenges as AI Technology Evolves

As AI technology evolves, so too do the ethical considerations that accompany its integration into business operations. The rapidly advancing capabilities of AI, including tools like ChatGPT, raise complex ethical questions that require careful navigation to ensure responsible and ethical usage. This section explores the evolving landscape of AI ethics and the strategies businesses can employ to address these challenges.

Understanding the Ethical Landscape:

As AI becomes more ingrained in daily business operations, understanding the ethical implications is paramount. Businesses must grapple with questions about biases in AI algorithms, data privacy, transparency, accountability, and the potential socioeconomic impact of widespread automation.

Continuous Ethical Assessment:

The evolving nature of AI technology means that ethical considerations are not static. Regularly assessing how AI integration aligns with ethical standards and societal values is essential. Businesses should be prepared to update their policies and practices as new ethical challenges arise.

Transparency and Accountability:

Transparency is key to maintaining user trust. Businesses should be transparent about when users are interacting with AI and clearly communicate the AI's limitations. Additionally, accountability mechanisms must be in place to address unintended consequences and errors stemming from AI-generated content.

Data Privacy and Security:

As AI relies on data, ensuring data privacy and security is paramount. Businesses must uphold stringent data protection measures to prevent unauthorized access, breaches, and misuse of user information.

Mitigating Bias and Fairness:

AI models, including ChatGPT, can inadvertently inherit biases present in training data. Businesses must actively mitigate bias and ensure fairness by employing diverse and representative data, conducting regular bias audits, and implementing fairness-aware algorithms.

Human Oversight and Intervention:

Human oversight remains crucial. Businesses should have mechanisms in place for human intervention when AI encounters challenges or produces content that raises ethical concerns.

Ethical Guidelines and Training:

Creating clear ethical guidelines and providing training for employees working with AI can help ensure that ethical considerations are consistently integrated into business operations.

Collaboration with Ethical Experts:

Collaborating with ethicists, researchers, and other experts can provide businesses with valuable insights into navigating ethical challenges. Cross-disciplinary collaboration enhances the ethical framework guiding AI integration.

Stakeholder Engagement:

Engaging with stakeholders, including customers and the wider public, fosters transparency and ensures that AI practices align with societal expectations.

As AI technology evolves, ethical considerations take center stage. Businesses that navigate these challenges with transparency, accountability, and a commitment to responsible AI integration will not only mitigate risks but also foster trust, reputation, and positive societal impact. By actively addressing ethical considerations, businesses can harness AI's potential while upholding their commitment to ethical principles in an ever-changing technological landscape.

Ensuring Ongoing Responsible and Transparent AI Usage

In the dynamic landscape of AI integration, ensuring ongoing responsible and transparent usage is a cornerstone of maintaining trust, adhering to ethical standards, and maximizing the benefits of AI technology. As businesses continue to leverage AI, including tools like ChatGPT, they must prioritize responsible practices that align with societal values and regulatory frameworks. This section delves into strategies for maintaining responsible and transparent AI usage.

Clear Ethical Guidelines:

Establishing clear and comprehensive ethical guidelines is foundational. These guidelines should outline principles, expectations, and best practices for AI usage within the organization. Regularly revisiting and updating these guidelines ensures they remain aligned with evolving ethical standards.

Governance and Oversight:

Creating dedicated governance structures and oversight mechanisms is crucial. Designating responsible teams or individuals to monitor AI usage, address ethical concerns, and implement corrective actions guarantees accountability.

Transparency in Communication:

Transparency builds trust. Businesses should openly communicate the presence of AI in customer interactions. Users should be aware when they are engaging with AI-driven systems to foster transparency and avoid deception.

User Education:

Educating users about the capabilities and limitations of AI interactions is essential. Providing guidance on how to interact effectively with AI systems empowers users and enhances their understanding of what to expect.

Regular Audits and Assessments:

Periodic audits of AI systems ensure compliance with ethical guidelines and data privacy regulations. These audits identify potential biases, inaccuracies, or unintended consequences and enable corrective actions.

Bias Mitigation and Fairness:

Employing measures to mitigate bias and ensure fairness is critical. Regularly reviewing training data, testing for bias, and employing techniques to address bias help prevent discriminatory outcomes.

Human Oversight:

Maintaining human oversight over AI-generated content is pivotal. Having humans review and approve critical content ensures that ethical standards are upheld and errors are minimized.

Feedback Loops:

Creating channels for users to provide feedback on AI interactions fosters a collaborative approach. Businesses can refine AI systems based on user feedback, ensuring continuous improvement.

Compliance with Regulations:

Remaining compliant with relevant regulations and data privacy laws is non-negotiable. Businesses must actively monitor changes in the legal landscape and adjust their AI practices accordingly.

Ethical Training:

Educating employees about ethical considerations in AI usage cultivates a culture of responsible AI integration. Training ensures that all members of the organization understand and prioritize ethical practices.

8. The Role of AI in ChatGPT for Business

Natural Language Processing (NLP) Basics

In the world of AI, Natural Language Processing (NLP) stands as a foundational pillar that empowers ChatGPT and similar models to excel in understanding and generating human language. This chapter delves into the essential principles of NLP and explores how its application drives the capabilities of ChatGPT in the business context.

Understanding Human Language:

NLP is the science of enabling computers to comprehend, interpret, and generate human language in a way that bridges the gap between human communication and machine processing. It encompasses a range of tasks, from text analysis and sentiment detection to language translation and speech recognition.

Components of NLP:

NLP comprises several core components that collectively enable AI systems to navigate the intricacies of language:

Tokenization: Breaking down text into smaller units, called tokens, such as words or subwords. This enables computers to analyze and process text effectively.

Part-of-Speech Tagging: Identifying the grammatical parts of speech (noun, verb, adjective, etc.) of each token, aiding in understanding sentence structure.

Named Entity Recognition (NER): Identifying entities like names of people, places, organizations, and dates in text, which is crucial for context comprehension.

Sentiment Analysis: Determining the emotional tone of text, whether it's positive, negative, or neutral. This aids in understanding user sentiment and responses.

Language Translation: Converting text from one language to another, facilitating global communication and market expansion.

Role of NLP in ChatGPT:

ChatGPT's prowess in understanding and generating human-like responses stems from its NLP foundation. NLP algorithms analyze input text, tokenize it, comprehend its structure, and predict the most likely subsequent words, creating coherent and contextually relevant responses.

NLP for Business:

In the business context, NLP opens doors to diverse applications. From understanding customer feedback and sentiment analysis for market insights to automating customer support and generating personalized content, NLP-powered AI like ChatGPT transforms how businesses engage with customers, streamline operations, and extract actionable insights.

Challenges in NLP:

While NLP has made remarkable strides, it faces challenges such as context comprehension, handling nuances in language, and overcoming language barriers. Businesses must be cognizant of these challenges to leverage NLP effectively.

Natural Language Processing is the bedrock on which AI-powered language models like ChatGPT thrive. Its ability to decode, comprehend, and generate human language is pivotal in redefining business interactions, insights, and innovation. Understanding NLP basics is a stepping stone toward harnessing the full potential of AI in ChatGPT for business applications.

Explaining NLP and its Importance in Chatbot Functionality

Natural Language Processing (NLP) is the backbone of chatbot functionality, enabling machines to understand, interpret, and generate human language. NLP's significance lies in its ability to bridge the gap between human communication nuances and the capabilities of AI-driven systems like chatbots.

Understanding NLP:

NLP is a multidisciplinary field that combines linguistics, computer science, and artificial intelligence. Its goal is to empower machines to comprehend and interact with human language in a way that feels natural and intuitive. NLP algorithms process textual data, breaking it down into smaller components, extracting meaning, and responding appropriately.

Components of NLP in Chatbots:

Tokenization: NLP begins by tokenizing text into units like words or subwords. This process allows the machine to understand the building blocks of language.

Language Structure: NLP helps machines understand the grammatical structure of sentences, identifying parts of speech and relationships between words.

Contextual Understanding: NLP enables chatbots to interpret the context of conversations. It understands the flow of conversation, remembers previous interactions, and generates responses that make sense within that context.

Named Entity Recognition: Chatbots can identify entities like names, dates, and locations in user input, enhancing their ability to provide relevant responses.

Sentiment Analysis: NLP allows chatbots to analyze the sentiment behind user messages, helping them respond appropriately to emotional cues.

Importance of NLP in Chatbot Functionality:

NLP is paramount for chatbots to deliver effective and human-like interactions:

User-Centric Engagement: NLP enables chatbots to understand user intent, ensuring they provide accurate and relevant responses, enhancing user satisfaction.

Conversational Flow: Chatbots with NLP can maintain the flow of conversations, understanding follow-up questions and maintaining context over extended interactions.

Personalization: By comprehending user preferences and context, chatbots can tailor responses, providing personalized experiences akin to one-on-one human interactions.

Language Diversity: NLP equips chatbots to engage users in different languages and dialects, expanding their reach in global markets.

Efficient Customer Support: NLP-powered chatbots automate routine customer queries, offering quick and accurate solutions while freeing up human agents for more complex issues.

Data Insights: NLP enables chatbots to analyze and extract valuable insights from customer interactions, contributing to market research, trend analysis, and customer behavior understanding.

NLP serves as the cognitive engine that empowers chatbots to communicate effectively with humans. By understanding user intent, maintaining context, and generating coherent responses, NLP-driven chatbots elevate customer engagement, streamline business operations, and open doors to innovative customer experiences. In the modern business landscape, where customer interaction is pivotal, NLP's role in chatbot functionality cannot be overstated.

How ChatGPT Understands and Generates Human-Like Text

ChatGPT's remarkable ability to understand and generate human-like text is rooted in its advanced Natural Language Processing (NLP) capabilities. This section delves into the intricacies of how ChatGPT comprehends and produces text that mimics human language, revolutionizing interactions in the business landscape.

Transformers and Self-Attention:

At the core of ChatGPT's operation lies the transformer architecture, a revolutionary model in NLP. Transformers use self-attention mechanisms to analyze relationships between words in a sentence, capturing dependencies regardless of their positions. This enables the model to understand context and nuances, critical for generating coherent responses.

Training with Context:

ChatGPT is trained on massive datasets containing diverse conversations. This training exposes the model to a wide range of language patterns, styles, and topics. Through exposure to context-rich interactions, ChatGPT learns to associate words, anticipate responses, and grasp conversational flow.

Tokenization and Embeddings:

When a user input is received, ChatGPT tokenizes it, breaking it down into manageable units. These tokens are then embedded into a numerical format that the model understands. This embedding retains semantic meaning, allowing the model to process and analyze the text.

Generating Responses:

Generating responses involves predicting the next set of tokens that form a coherent sentence. Given an input, ChatGPT's self-attention mechanisms weigh the importance of each token based on its relationship with others. This attention mechanism helps the model focus on relevant context and generate a contextually appropriate response.

Contextual Understanding:

ChatGPT doesn't merely generate responses in isolation; it considers the entire conversation. It maintains a short-term memory of the conversation history, allowing it to grasp the ongoing context, recall previous turns, and ensure its responses align with the flow of the conversation.

Incorporating Diversity:

ChatGPT's training data include a variety of writing styles, tones, and topics. This diversity equips the model to respond in ways that mirror the variability of human expression, making its outputs more natural and engaging.

Fine-Tuning for Specific Tasks:

After pretraining on a broad range of data, ChatGPT can be fine-tuned for specific tasks or industries. This involves training the model on narrower datasets, guiding it to generate contextually relevant content tailored to the business's needs.

ChatGPT's ability to understand and generate human-like text is a testament to the advancements in NLP and AI. By utilizing transformer architectures, training on diverse datasets, and considering context, ChatGPT brings about a paradigm shift in communication between businesses and their customers. As organizations embrace this technology, they unlock the potential to revolutionize customer interactions, content generation, and the way they engage with their target audience.

Continuous Learning and Improvement

Training Chatbots with New Data for Better Performance

In the ever-evolving landscape of AI, continuous learning and improvement play a pivotal role in enhancing the performance of chatbots like ChatGPT. This section delves into the importance of training chatbots with new data and how businesses can leverage this practice to elevate the capabilities of their AI-driven interactions.

The Need for Continuous Learning:

Chatbots are not static entities; they can adapt and grow with new information. The inclusion of fresh data is essential to refine their responses, incorporate the latest trends, and adapt to changing user preferences and language nuances.

Diverse and Relevant Data:

Training chatbots with a diverse range of data sources is crucial. This data diversity exposes the chatbot to various writing styles, contexts, and industry-specific language, enabling it to generate more accurate and contextually relevant responses.

User Feedback Integration:

User feedback is a goldmine of insights for chatbot enhancement. Businesses can gather feedback on interactions, analyze it, and use it to fine-tune the chatbot's responses. This iterative feedback loop ensures that the chatbot aligns better with user expectations over time.

Fine-Tuning for Specific Domains:

Businesses can enhance chatbot performance by fine-tuning it for specific domains or industries. By providing targeted training data and guidance, the chatbot becomes more proficient in addressing industry-specific queries and generating domain-relevant content.

Balancing Automation and Human Oversight:

While automated learning is essential, human oversight is equally critical. Businesses should closely monitor the chatbot's interactions, correct any misinterpretations, and provide guidance to improve its responses. This synergy between AI and human input refines the chatbot's performance.

Managing Bias and Ethical Considerations:

Introducing new data requires careful consideration to avoid reinforcing biases or generating inappropriate content. Businesses must ensure that the training data is representative and aligns with ethical guidelines, preventing the chatbot from producing biased or offensive responses.

Incorporating Real-Time Trends:

Training chatbots with new data enables them to stay current with real-time trends. This agility equips them to respond to emerging topics and industry developments promptly, enhancing their value in providing up-to-date information.

The journey of training chatbots with new data is a commitment to continuous improvement. By staying receptive to user feedback, incorporating diverse and relevant information, and fine-tuning for specific domains, businesses can elevate their chatbots' performance. In a world where user expectations evolve rapidly, chatbots that embrace continuous learning not only meet user needs effectively but also forge lasting relationships by delivering exceptional and contextually accurate AI-powered interactions.

Addressing Limitations and Refining Responses Over Time

The evolution of AI-powered chatbots is a dynamic process that involves addressing limitations and continuously refining responses. This section explores the importance of recognizing and overcoming limitations while leveraging ongoing improvement to optimize chatbot interactions in the business context.

Recognizing Limitations:

Every chatbot, including ChatGPT, has inherent limitations. These might include generating inaccurate responses, misinterpreting context, or struggling with complex queries. Acknowledging these limitations is the first step toward improving chatbot performance.

Iterative Learning Process:

Addressing limitations is an iterative process. By analyzing user interactions, identifying recurring issues, and understanding where the chatbot falls short, businesses can develop strategies to fine-tune its responses and capabilities.

User Feedback Integration:

User feedback is a valuable resource for refining chatbot responses. Businesses should actively encourage users to provide feedback, whether positive or negative, and use this input to make necessary adjustments and improvements.

Human Oversight and Correction:

Human oversight plays a crucial role in refining chatbot responses. When the chatbot generates inaccurate or inappropriate content, human intervention can correct the output and guide the chatbot toward more accurate responses in the future.

Fine-Tuning with Targeted Data:

Fine-tuning involves training the chatbot on specific datasets relevant to the business domain. By exposing the chatbot to focused data, it can better understand industry-specific language, context, and user preferences, leading to more accurate and relevant responses.

Regular Updates and Training:

Regularly updating and retraining the chatbot with new data prevents stagnation. As language evolves and user behavior changes, consistent training ensures the chatbot remains aligned with current trends and user expectations.

Managing Bias and Sensitivity:

Chatbots must navigate potential biases and sensitive topics responsibly. Businesses should invest in continuous monitoring to identify and rectify biased or inappropriate responses, minimizing potential harm.

Ethical Considerations:

Refining responses should always adhere to ethical guidelines. Ensuring that the chatbot generates content that is respectful, unbiased, and aligned with user values builds trust and safeguards the reputation of the business.

Feedback-Driven Innovation:

A feedback-driven approach to refining responses fosters innovation. As businesses act on user feedback, they not only enhance the chatbot's capabilities but also demonstrate a commitment to customer satisfaction and continuous improvement.

Conclusion

The process of refining chatbot responses is a journey that requires vigilance, user-centricity, and adaptability. By addressing limitations, incorporating user feedback, and fine-tuning the chatbot's capabilities, businesses can optimize interactions, foster user engagement, and create a positive impact on customer experiences. As AI technology evolves, the commitment to refining responses over time is integral to achieving AI-powered interactions that align with business goals and deliver exceptional value.

Ethical Considerations and Data Privacy

Ensuring Responsible AI Usage and User Data Protection

In the world of AI-powered chatbots, ethical considerations and data privacy are paramount. This section delves into the critical importance of ensuring responsible AI usage and safeguarding user data, highlighting the strategies that businesses must adopt to uphold ethical standards and protect user privacy.

Responsible AI Usage:

Businesses integrating AI, including chatbots, must prioritize ethical considerations:

Bias Mitigation: AI models can inherit biases from training data, resulting in biased or discriminatory responses. Regular bias assessments, data curation, and algorithmic fairness measures are vital to ensure AI-generated content is unbiased and equitable.

Transparency: Users should be informed that they are interacting with an AI-powered chatbot. Transparent communication sets the right expectations and builds trust.

Content Moderation: Implement robust content moderation to prevent the generation of offensive or inappropriate content. Human oversight and moderation mechanisms are necessary to ensure the chatbot's outputs align with ethical standards.

User Consent: Users must consent to interacting with AI and the storage of their data. Clearly articulate the purpose of data collection and usage to foster transparency and user trust.

User Data Protection:

Safeguarding user data is a non-negotiable responsibility:

Data Minimization: Collect only necessary user data and avoid excessive data gathering. Limit the scope of data collected to protect user privacy.

Secure Storage: Employ robust encryption and security measures to protect stored user data from unauthorized access and breaches.

Data Sharing: Never share user data with third parties without explicit user consent. Respect user privacy and honor data sharing preferences.

Anonymization: Whenever possible, anonymize user data to prevent the identification of individual users. This enhances data privacy while allowing for meaningful analysis.

Compliance with Regulations:

Adhering to data protection regulations is essential:

GDPR (General Data Protection Regulation): If operating in the European Union, comply with GDPR's stringent data protection rules, including user consent, data access rights, and breach reporting.

CCPA (California Consumer Privacy Act): If dealing with California residents, adhere to CCPA's requirements regarding user data rights and privacy disclosures.

Regular Audits and Assessments:

Continuously assess AI systems' compliance with ethical standards and data privacy regulations:

Data Impact Assessments: Conduct assessments to evaluate potential risks to user data and privacy, and take steps to mitigate these risks.

External Audits: Engage external auditors to assess AI systems for ethical considerations and data privacy compliance.

Education and User Empowerment:

Educate users about data privacy practices:

Privacy Policies: Clearly articulate data collection, usage, and retention policies in easily accessible privacy statements.

User Controls: Empower users with controls over their data, including the ability to opt out of data collection or request data deletion.

Incorporating responsible AI usage and data privacy principles into chatbot operations is a moral obligation and a strategic imperative. By respecting ethical considerations, safeguarding user data, complying with regulations, and promoting transparency, businesses not only build trust with their users but also contribute to a safer and more ethical AI ecosystem. In the pursuit of innovation, responsible AI usage and data privacy must remain unwavering priorities.

Mitigating Biases and Maintaining Ethical Standards

Maintaining ethical standards and mitigating biases are critical cornerstones when integrating AI-powered chatbots into business operations. This section delves into the importance of addressing biases and upholding ethical principles, providing strategies for businesses to ensure that their AI interactions are fair, unbiased, and aligned with ethical considerations.

Understanding Bias in AI:

Bias in AI can emerge from biased training data, perpetuating stereotypes and discrimination. It's imperative to recognize that AI systems like chatbots can unintentionally amplify societal biases, leading to unfair or offensive content generation.

Identifying Biased Outputs:

Constant monitoring and human oversight are essential to identify biased outputs. Reviewing chatbot responses and interactions can help identify instances where biases might manifest, allowing for immediate correction and improvement.

Diverse and Representative Training Data:

Curating diverse and representative training data is crucial. A broader range of data helps minimize biases and ensures that the chatbot is exposed to various perspectives, languages, cultures, and contexts.

Bias Mitigation Algorithms:

AI models can be fine-tuned with bias mitigation algorithms. These algorithms work to reduce biased responses by penalizing or altering outputs that exhibit biases, ultimately guiding the model toward more equitable content generation.

Human-in-the-Loop Approach:

Integrating a human-in-the-loop approach ensures human reviewers validate and refine AI-generated content. This ongoing collaboration helps catch biases, correct inaccuracies, and maintain ethical standards.

Clear Guidelines and Policies:

Establishing clear guidelines for content generation is vital. Businesses must provide specific instructions to the AI model, reinforcing ethical boundaries and preventing the generation of content that violates these principles.

Regular Bias Audits:

Conducting regular bias audits involves assessing the AI model's outputs for any biased or discriminatory content. These audits ensure that any biases are identified and corrected promptly.

User Feedback and Reporting Mechanisms:

Empower users to report biased or inappropriate content generated by the chatbot. User feedback plays a pivotal role in identifying biases and refining the AI model.

Ethical Review Boards:

Establishing ethical review boards or committees can provide oversight for AI-powered systems. These boards evaluate the chatbot's outputs from an ethical standpoint, making recommendations for improvement.

Transparency and Accountability:

Maintain transparency about the measures taken to mitigate biases. Demonstrating a commitment to ethical standards fosters user trust and confidence in AI-powered interactions.

Mitigating biases and maintaining ethical standards are foundational to responsible AI integration. Businesses that prioritize these considerations not only ensure fair and equitable interactions but also contribute to a more inclusive digital landscape. By implementing strategies to minimize biases, collaborating with human reviewers, and fostering transparency, businesses can harness the full potential of AI while safeguarding against biases that could undermine the integrity of their AI-driven interactions.

Conclusion

In the rapidly evolving landscape of business, the integration of AI-powered chatbots, such as ChatGPT, has emerged as a transformative force. This book has journeyed through the myriad dimensions of leveraging ChatGPT for business operations, offering insights into its capabilities, applications, ethical considerations, and future prospects. As we conclude this exploration, let's reflect on the profound impact that ChatGPT can have on businesses and the way they engage with customers, streamline operations, and drive innovation.

ChatGPT, with its Natural Language Processing capabilities, enables businesses to create personalized customer engagements, automate content generation, streamline customer support, and delve into data-driven insights. The benefits of this technology are vast—improved user experiences, enhanced operational efficiency, data-driven decision-making, and the potential for new revenue streams.

Yet, with great power comes great responsibility. Ethical considerations and data privacy must be at the forefront of AI integration. Businesses must navigate potential biases, ensure transparent communication about AI usage, safeguard user data, and adhere to regulatory guidelines. By embracing responsible AI usage and continuous learning, businesses can foster trust, mitigate biases, and create AI-powered interactions that genuinely resonate with users.

As AI continues to evolve, its role in reshaping industries and business landscapes is undeniable. The book has delved into the potential AI holds across various sectors, predicting how it will shape e-commerce, healthcare, finance, and more. The integration of AI isn't just about staying current; it's about future-proofing businesses, optimizing processes, and staying ahead in an era defined by digital innovation.

Ultimately, the journey of integrating ChatGPT into business operations is marked by innovation, adaptation, and an unwavering commitment to delivering value to customers. As businesses embrace the possibilities offered by AI-powered chatbots, they pave the way for a future where human and machine collaboration becomes the norm, enhancing customer experiences and driving business success.

This book has provided a comprehensive overview of ChatGPT's applications, ethical considerations, and strategic integration. It is our hope that the insights shared here will serve as a guide for businesses venturing into the world of AI-powered interactions. The potential is vast, the opportunities are exciting, and the future holds the promise of a harmonious coexistence between AI and human-driven business endeavors.

As you embark on this journey, keep in mind the following key takeaways:

Understanding the Power of AI: Recognize the capabilities of ChatGPT and how it can elevate various aspects of your business, from customer engagement to content generation and beyond.

Ethical Considerations: Place ethical considerations at the forefront. Uphold transparency, mitigate biases, and safeguard user data to ensure responsible AI usage.

Continuous Learning: Embrace continuous learning as a guiding principle. Regularly update your chatbot with new data, refine responses, and adapt to evolving user preferences.

User-Centric Approach: Keep the user experience at the center of your AI integration strategy. Align AI interactions with user expectations, personalize content, and actively seek user feedback.

Collaboration Between AI and Humans: Embrace the collaborative nature of AI-human interaction. Human oversight, feedback integration, and responsible human intervention are essential for refining AI-generated content.

Strategic Integration: Integrate ChatGPT strategically within your business processes. From marketing and customer support to generating revenue streams, align AI integration with your organizational goals.

Future Outlook: Anticipate the future trends in AI and business. Embrace AI as a transformative force that will continue to reshape industries and create new possibilities.

As you navigate the complex terrain of AI integration, remember that ChatGPT is a tool—a powerful one—but the true magic happens when it's harnessed with empathy, insight, and strategic vision. AI's potential to revolutionize the way businesses operate is within reach, and the journey you embark upon today will define the trajectory of your business in the years to come. With responsible AI usage, a commitment to ethical standards, and an unwavering dedication to delivering value to your customers, the future is bright, innovative, and full of possibilities. Embrace the future, embrace AI, and forge a path toward success that's powered by the fusion of human ingenuity and technological advancement.

Finally, if you enjoyed this book, please take the time to share your thoughts and post a review on Amazon. It'd be greatly appreciated!

Thank you and good luck!

www.ingramcontent.com/pod-product-compliance
Lightning Source LLC
LaVergne TN
LVHW082356200926
848481LV00012B/3587